Nam

SELECT

A.C. JACOBS

A.C. (Arthur) Jacobs was born in Glasgow into an Orthodox Jewish family in 1937 and grew up under the shadow of the Holocaust. An erudite and committed poet from a young age, he became a self-made migrant, a wanderer through countries and through other people's more settled lives. He was a Jew in Scotland, a Scot in England, and a diaspora Jew wherever he traveled. *Nameless Country* returns selections of A.C. Jacobs' poetry to a 21st-century audience. His poems compel our attention because they bear the stamp of their long-ago moment but in their embrace of complex identities, speak clearly to our own.

Merle L. Bachman is an American Jewish poet with two full-length collections published by Shearsman Books in the UK: *Diorama with Fleeing Figures* and *Blood Party*. In addition to her scholarly work on A.C. Jacobs, she works in the field of American Yiddish literature. Syracuse University Press published her monograph, *Recovering 'Yiddishland': Threshold Moments in American Literature*. In 2015 she was a Translation Fellow of the Massachusetts-based Yiddish Book Center. Bachman is a Professor of English at Spalding University in Louisville, Kentucky.

Anthony Rudolf is a poet, memoirist, translator and retired publisher. Menard Press, which he founded in 1969, co-published *Collected Poems & Selected Translations* of A.C. Jacobs and published two other books by him. Rudolf's own collected poems, *European Hours*, were published by Carcanet Press in 2017. His most recent memoir, *Silent Conversations: A Reader's Life*, was published by Seagull Books in 2013. And his book about his cousin Jerzy Feliks Urman, *Jerzyk*, the only known child suicide of the Holocaust, was published by Shearsman Books in 2017. He lives in London.

Arthur C. Jacobs.
Alyth. 4 April 1980

Nameless Country

SELECTED POEMS OF
A.C. JACOBS

edited by Merle L. Bachman and Anthony Rudolf

Northern House

CARCANET

Other Works by A.C. Jacobs

Collected Poems & Selected Translations, edited by John Rety and
Anthony Rudolf (Menard Press/Hearing Eye)
Poems by Avraham ben Yitzhak (Tim Gee Editions)
The Proper Blessing (Menard Press)
The Dark Gate: Poems of David Vogel (Menard Press)
A Bit of Dialect (Hearing Eye Press; Torriano Poetry Pamphlets #1)

First published in Great Britain in 2018 by
Northern House
in association Carcanet Press Ltd
Alliance House, 30 Cross Street
Manchester M2 7AQ
www.carcanet.co.uk

MIX
Paper from
responsible sources
FSC
www.fsc.org   FSC® C014540

A CIP catalogue record for this book is available from the British Library.
ISBN 978 1 78410 675 1

The publisher acknowledges financial assistance from Arts Council England

Supported by
**ARTS COUNCIL
ENGLAND**

and from the Stand Magazine Support Trust

Typeset in England by XL Publishing Services, Exmouth
Printed and bound in England by SRP Ltd, Exeter

Contents

1 Early Poems

2 From The Proper Blessing

3 *From* A Bit of Dialect

4 '… *cold diasporas*…'

Acknowledgements

The Editors gratefully acknowledge the permission of Sheila Gilbert, Literary Executor to A.C. Jacobs' estate, to publish the work herein, including archival materials.

The Editors also wish to thank Ms. Joanne C. Fitton, Head of Special Collections, and the staff of Special Collections in the Brotherton Library at the University of Leeds, where the Archive of A.C. Jacobs' work is located. They kindly provided the photographs of manuscript material used herein, which can be found on pp. 2, 16, 50, 68 and 94. These materials are from MS 2065/1, Boxes 2 and 5 and are reproduced with the permission of Special Collections, Leeds University Library.

The Editors also gratefully acknowledge Sheila Gilbert for providing and permitting the publication herein of selected photos of A.C. Jacobs from her personal archive, which can be seen on pp. 1, 15, 43, 49, 67 and 93. Further, we thank Gerald Mangan for permitting the publication of his sketch of A.C. Jacobs as the book's Frontispiece as well as the photo he took of Jacobs that appears on p. 44.

★

In addition, Merle Bachman adds:

I wish to thank Sheila, Arthur's sister, for her kindness in allowing visits to Arthur's archive when it was still located in her home, and both Sheila and her husband Geoffrey Gilbert for conversation, cups of tea, lifts to the tube station and, in general, their interested support in the research that led to this book. Deep thanks and gratitude also to Anthony Rudolf, without whom I would never have met Sheila, and for being such a wise, encouraging and supportive colleague from the very beginning.

Further thanks go to Spalding University for professional development funding that helped cover the costs of travel; to Peter Lawson and the Open University for accepting my paper on A.C. Jacobs' 'diasporic poetics' for the *British Jewish: Contemporary Culture* conference in July 2015, and then publishing it in article form in the July 2016 issue of *The Journal of European Popular Culture* (7:1); and to Alan Golding (University of Louisville) and Kathryn Hellerstein (University of Pennsylvania) for important conversations, and to Shachar Pinsker (University of Michigan), for my talk at the Frankel Center for Judaic Studies in Fall 2015, half of which was on Jacobs' poetry.

Introduction

Merle L. Bachman

1 A Man in Motion

While still a young man, the poet Arthur (A.C.) Jacobs wrote:

I could conceive of my life as no more than sequences of journeys, or perhaps journey within journey (archive).

Arthur Jacobs began his journeys in Glasgow, Scotland, where he was born in 1937 into an Orthodox Jewish family. His grandparents had done their own travelling, emigrating towards America from Lithuania, and finding themselves content to stay in Scotland. Arthur's family moved to London, however, when he was a young teenager – one who was already beginning to regard himself as a writer. Growing to adulthood in England, yet holding fast to a Scottish identity, added another layer to the precocious poet's sense of himself, as did his own travel to Israel, where he lived for three formative years in the early 1960s. When Arthur left for Israel, he had already forsaken the religious practices of Jewish orthodoxy, but he remained enmeshed all his life with Jewishness – its languages, history, and intellectual culture. The gift of his time in Israel was, ironically, that it sharpened his commitment to being a diaspora Jew with 'access to three or four cultures'* – one who came to know modern Hebrew well enough that he could make a partial living from translating the work of Israeli writers.

After Israel, barely 30 years of age, he gave himself a middle name – 'Chaim,' the Hebrew word for *life* – and began to sign his poem drafts, 'A.C. Jacobs.'

Journey within journey. *I wanted to go to Edinburgh. The puzzle of Scotland moves me more than any other like it… Greyness and lost vigour. Very well, I am a romantic. A two thousand year old nostalgia seeps its melancholy through my veins…* (archive). From Israel to London to

---

* From the poem 'Israeli Arab' (p. 79).

Edinburgh, to the Scottish Borders, to London, and back again – his movement continued, interspersed with travels to Italy and especially Spain, the country that kindled in him new excitements, new perspectives on Jewish history. Jacobs' choice in life as well as in writing was to remain at the borders, ever an insider/outsider, to reject 'settling' or settling down. While his restlessness might have cost him the sustained focus necessary to extend his body of work, it also fed the internal tensions expressed in his most powerful poems. His poetic persona is one that embraces the facts of his own marginality, as a Jew in Scotland, a Scot in England, an 'Anglo-Saxon' in Israel, and a diaspora Jew everywhere.

It was in Madrid, in 1994, at the seeming cusp of a new phase, that Jacobs' journeys came to an end. He died suddenly, shortly before his 57th birthday.

Poetry, of course, has the capacity to live on. Over time, Jacobs had garnered poet colleagues, supporters and friends, starting when he'd been a young participant in meetings of Philip Hobsbaum's 'Group' when it was based in north London. The poet Jon Silkin became an important mentor and friend. His poems and translations had appeared in a number of journals, including *Stand* and *Ambit*, and in two anthologies. Two modest collections of his work had been published: *The Proper Blessing* (his own poems) and *The Dark Gate* (translations from David Vogel), both in 1976, by Anthony Rudolf's Menard Press. Tim Gee Editions also republished an expanded version of *The Proper Blessing* in 1992 and came out with a posthumous edition of Jacobs' translations from Avraham Ben-Yitzhak, later in 1994. After Jacobs' untimely death, a big surprise was in store for his poetry community: scattered throughout his files and folders lay almost *twice* the number of his published poems, nearly all of them finished, and many of them extraordinary. This motivated the publication in 1996 (again by Menard Press, co-published with John Rety's Hearing Eye Press) of Jacobs' *Collected Poems and Selected Translations*, co-edited by Rudolf and Rety.

And, years later, my own discovery of the *Collected* set in motion a chain of events that has led to the volume at hand. The *Selected Poems* is intended to bring Arthur's distinctive perspectives and quiet, questioning voice into a new moment, before a new audience, with hopes that the poems will be off on fresh travels.

So much of what stays present of a human life, if not committed to memory or to paper, is subject to uncertainty. Was this poet more 'English' or more 'Scottish'? He certainly was always Jewish. What were the real-life reasons for his travels? Were they for love or seeking out work to cobble together a life, or to shake up the conditions that exacerbated his intermittent ill health (due to asthma)? Or did he travel to relieve the pressure of internal discomforts with the quotidian, the mundane? He had no university degree, though he did spend time in the mid-1970s studying at the Oxford Centre for Hebrew and Jewish Studies. His primary work was in translation. How did he manage translating poems and fiction written by Israeli authors, while pursuing his own creative work? The drafts of correspondence one finds in his archive point up anxieties related to all these things, but his scattered journal jottings and essay drafts indicate a confidence in his own intellectual engagement with a literary and Jewish world that extended outward from wherever he temporarily situated himself.

Unlike my co-editor, Anthony Rudolf, I never knew Arthur; the interests that would bring me to Scotland and to his poetry had not yet revealed themselves to me in the early 1990s, when I was an MFA student in Oakland, California. My acquaintance with Arthur comes through his poems and a number of visits to Sheila Gilbert, Arthur's younger sister and literary executor, who had until recently kept the poet's modest archive in her London home. On one of my visits to look through the archive, she said what a shame it was that I couldn't have met him. I could only reply with my enthusiasm for his writing. But handling the onion-skin paper he sometimes had used for typing up drafts, noting a coffee stain, the brown corona of a dropped cigarette ash, made Arthur real to me. I felt a deep connection to him as a fellow wanderer and poet, a lover of Scottish hills and a Jew rooted (if that can even be said) in diaspora.

Ultimately, of course, it's the work itself that insists on our attention. And his compelling poems deserve this reintroduction.

As is the case with any poet no longer living, even from the recent past, their poems bring a lost world with them. However, the particular 20th century world in which Arthur Jacobs grew up may seem distant. It is a world in which war could be cast as simply good against evil, where the Holocaust still threw its sharp, grim shadow, and where a Jewish state could come into being – as well as its powerful myths. 'It is time,' Arthur wrote at one point while living in Israel, 'to set down some thoughts about the confrontation of myself, a tiny poet in whom some of the threads of a vast condition of exile continue to quiver, with the landed nationalism of some of my people' [archive]. Until the end of his life, despite his increasing maturity and sophistication, it seems that Jacobs' poetry never lost this *feeling* of 'earliness' – that is, the consciousness of a young Jewish writer for whom diaspora is not a dead concept but one charged with ongoing relevance, historically and personally.

Jacobs' poems compel on many levels, because, in addition to their unique aesthetic, they do 'cultural work.' That is, they serve as a potential center of inquiry into what it meant to be a Jew in the 20th century: especially one who writes about Israel but chooses not to live there. Among the most significant posthumous discoveries in Arthur's poems are the ones about Israel that could not appear in *The Proper Blessing*. I refer you to poems such as 'Israeli Arab,' 'Bab El Wad,' and 'To a Teacher of Hebrew Literature,' which reopen for us uncomfortable yet essential questions about the Israel-diaspora relationship, at a time when such reflections might otherwise seem foreclosed.

Jacobs' love for Scotland as well as his ambivalent connection to England also form the ground of his poetry. In poems such as 'Introduction to a Scottish Sequence,' 'A Joke Across the North Sea,' 'I Choose Neither,' and 'N.W. 2: Spring,' Jacobs enacts an interplay of cultural identities – Scottish and English as well as Jewish. He invites us experience identity as a layered, shifting awareness, 'split at the foot of several cultures.'* And while he was immersed, as a translator, in modern Hebrew, Jacobs himself claimed in a letter to John Rety that his 'real language [was] probably Scots-Yiddish.'† Such a dialect did exist when he was a child, and it was replicated in his poem 'Dear Mr Leonard' (p. 98).

Above all, in his poems, one finds that a sense of *exile* clings,

---

* 'To a Teacher of Hebrew Literature' (p. 90).
† From Anthony Rudolf's 'Introduction' to the *Collected Poems*.

not just belonging to Jewish history but to a man who created and guarded his own exile, even *within* the Jewish community to which he was both insider and outsider (as in the poem, 'Where', p. 33).

3   A Note on this Book's Structure

Some issues that relate to the presentation of Arthur's work have not altered since the publication of the *Collected*: for example, Arthur rarely dated his drafts. And the exact dates of his moves away and back to London, or of his involvement with particular translation projects, all of which could provide some illumination as to chronology, have proved difficult to track. A future visitor to the archive, which has now found a permanent home at the University of Leeds, may be able to work out a timeline in greater detail. What *is* clearer now is that Arthur's creative output in the 1980s seems to have been far less than that of the 1960s and 70s. The pamphlet, 'A Bit of Dialect,' published by Hearing Eye Press in 1991, consists of just ten poems. These were added to the 1992 republishing of *The Proper Blessing* (by Tim Gee Editions).

In this *Selected*, we have chosen to begin the book with poems that are among his earliest, most of which come from notebooks he kept in his late teenage years and of which just two were eventually published: 'Sovereign Penny' and 'On a Trip to York' (both in *Stand*). We then present selections from *The Proper Blessing*, followed by choices from the pamphlet (so as to emphasize its different focus to what appears in the core book). We follow with selections from the poems that had not been published during Arthur's lifetime. Here, we are arranging them thematically, because it appears that he had drafted many of them during and shortly after the years he spent in Israel. While it is not known when he completed them, their origins seem to be in the same time period (from his mid-20s through early 30s).

A final note: throughout, we have adhered to Arthur's scheme for capitalization and punctuation in his poems.

Background on the Collected Poems

Anthony Rudolf

The *Collected Poems & Selected Translations* of 1996 (co-edited and co-published by John Rety and myself) contains an entire apparatus of criticism, memoir and contextualisation, as well as full notes concerning details (including variants) in the poems and translations. Such an apparatus is not needed in a *Selected Poems*, which is intended to bring the poet's best work to a new audience, while reminding existing readers of his distinguished body of work. Those readers of the present volume who wish to find out more about Jacobs and read the rest of his previously published work can track down the *Collected* in libraries or on Amazon and other online platforms. A few copies remain in print at the time of writing.

The *Collected* includes essays by John Rety, Frederick Grubb, Philip Hobsbaum and Jon Silkin, all now deceased, as well as my own introduction and the speech I gave at Arthur's tombstone setting. About a third of the poems in the two hundred and fifty page book consists of translations from the Hebrew, in particular Avraham Ben-Yitzhak and David Vogel, but also Bialik and poets of a later generation, including Yehuda Amichai. Perhaps one day Jacobs' complete translations will be reprinted in a separate volume. Merle Bachman and I agreed that we should concentrate entirely on his own poetry, lest readers be distracted from that work by the translated masters, as has happened with other poet-translators such as Michael Hamburger, Daniel Weissbort and Keith Bosley, who were all well known to Arthur.

I conclude with two remarks from the *Collected Poems* which encourage meditation on A.C. Jacobs, the poet and the man: first, in a letter to Jacobs, the novelist Dan Jacobson refers to 'your northern Anglo-Scottish pragmatical self coming down hard on your more emotional Jewish self'. And from Jon Silkin's introductory essay: 'having a minority consciousness, [Jacobs] could site himself nowhere... except in his speech and written language'. Finally, in the poem titled 'Place' from *A Bit of Dialect*, one finds the poet himself awaiting redemption in his very own Vilna, 'a bit east of the Gorbals, / in around the heart.'

1
Early Poems

'… as if born in a different climate…'

In the narrow crowded streets
Of this cold northern town
I remember the elegies for the besieged martyrs
Of eight hundred years ago
nearly

And in the minster
Where the good archbishops lie in state .
I want to scream in Hebrew
Up the great square tower
And dance on the placid flagstones
Kissing the **CHAMBER OF TRADE**
For the death of one Jew

ORIGINAL GUIDE

But I stood and watched the choirboys, two by two,
In red and white moving to Evensong
The dead of York and Kiev and Warsaw
in the ghetto of **THE CITY OF**
Our words mourn them

YORK

Alien Poem

I was born in a strange land.
Though I never invoked strangeness
The houses' grey walls
Of the town that was chosen
Kept back secrets, because of my lateness.

And though my father remembered
Other towns with trams and trees and silence
Their secrets, too
Would not be shared
With vagabonds, however respectable.

Strangers never grow into cities,
And their children encumbered with memories
Are clumsy, and afraid
They miss too much.
Sometimes, the strangeness is itself a promise.

Langside

The grey cloak of the city
Loosens on this hill.
The summit, half proud, inhales
The air of battle,
And more ashamed sinks into memory.

A tall queen, sad and ghostly,
Sometimes mounts the wind
To her dearly tragic end,
But no echoes fall
On the street's formality of traffic.

This hill holds her spirit
Above the unmoved town
Of this strange slow dying land:
Too proud to keep a queen,
Too meek to serve its own wisdom.

Poem for Innocent Victims of War

You did not die for me
Or love or desperation.
No-one chipped your names
On plaques on peaceful blocks of stone.
You are just the useless dead
Who mock our daily sin of passion,
Climb through our heads in cold, slow silence.

When you were people
We could have loved you,
Found out your names
And brought you presents.
We could have walked around with your response.

Or even if you chose to die
We might have understood your longing
And written down your utmost fear.

Now, though, you have got beyond our feelings,
And we can never almost follow
To learn your last shared and perfect secret.

Poem to a Sick Woman

You never learned that suffering was an art:
How to convey the pain that roamed the acres
Of your hurt inside that everyone tried to avoid.
I suffer, you said, *and no one understands.*

Grief, like great love, requires some talent, which we
Mostly do not possess, unhappily imitate;
Being not lesser Christs but passing fools
Whose little martyrdoms are interesting, then bore.

I know you suffer in some bestial way,
Your body's poison rages on your peace,
But for these most you have my awkward sympathy –
The maimed words that stumble when you start to tell.

Poem for John Knox

A goading, rigid puritan,
You were most of the landscape.

And my grandfather, without formal recognition,
Must have met you many times.

He would have seen his children
Chipped and shaped by the harsh rigour of your words.

And wondered at the smell of debate
You spread among the trespassing city:

Though his dream of final revealed redemption
Could never be obliterated,
But flourished more in this jealous, acid soil.

You, too, would have made a garden here,
Though with mostly home-grown seed:
And certainly your roots have squirmed and stretched
And stiffened under the lashed earth.

I, sinning against my grandfather's messiah,
And the tang of restraint you imposed on my neighbours,
Remember and am consoled
By burd Helen and the loves of Robert Burns.

Towards a Grief

Sometimes a poem is a desecration of grief:
When our brave detachment from the act of love
Turns to a vicious instrument that rips
A hard and human passion to acceptable phrases.

I say now only that the eyes of her I love
Are swollen, and at times her voice trembles.
My knowledge of what she feels turns elsewhere,
These lines have nothing for either of us.

For Certain Immigrants

The lives you have come up
Out of, I have not yet begun to understand.

I observe your thin boned elegant hands
Your love of colour, and hear
With a strange pleasure
The inimitable gutturals of your speech.

I see also your limbs shrivelled in weird poverties,

And I hear you stumble in a dialect of exile
That learned less, I think, than ours
How grief and pity could be diagnosed
And set down calmly in a classic style.

Oy

Funny exclamation
Almost as if it were born in another climate
Driven out from mouths by a foreign wind.

Yet its dirty liquid sorrow
Wails in our streets and ruins our houses
As if the very walls had sinned.

And a brick conspiracy
Keeps the sound for eternal sighing
Though the gods who heard it only grinned.

Sovereign Penny

1

My grandfather, the benevolent head
On a penny, pressed in my scraped fist
Will not be twisted across
His round flat smiling world.

2

He crouches away from awkward holes
That have lost me many coins
Down in the hot hell of my pocket,
He won't suffocate.

3

This infinite well-wisher
Falls untouched through the steel
Throats of slot machines
Back into my bent hand.

4

Thrown to the sun, he spins
His grin back to the dust
And waits obtrusive
For me to pick him up.

5

I know what he wants:
To be a proud charm on a string round my neck.
When I tug at him for luck or breath
I'll choke.

The Infinite Scale

The books and scrolls of our suffering
Outweigh the huge stone image of our God
And elegies rise, with their sickness, in our throats
More surely than the wrapped, counted words of prayer.

It is terrible to walk under these mountains of suffering
For ties intrude outside the power of words.
When I suggest my love's least comfortable need
The round figure is formed of the destroyed.

I want to measure my wounds by those who have not gone
      so far in agonies,
To have a less knowledgeable conscience.
But such standards are not for me to make:
To be told, the massive guilt remains.

You

You creep like a hungry animal
Up to all my feasts of words,
And though you are always silent
I am troubled by your presence.

A guest whose need is not made known
Should want no sustenance
But you bring justice with your silence
And I must make provision

Since I have asked you once to stay
And you never replied, but waited
As if there were more formalities.
Speak, just, and tell me what I have omitted.

On a Trip to York

In 1190 there was a massacre of the Jews at York.

In the narrow, crowded streets
Of this cold northern town
I remember the elegies for the besieged martyrs
Of nearly eight hundred years ago.

And in the Minster, where
The good archbishops gently smile in stone,
I want to scream in Hebrew
Up the great square tower
And dance on the placid flagstones
Kicking at the scrupulous shock
For the death of one improbable Jew.

But I stand and watch the choirboys, two by two,
In red and white, marching to evensong,

And think: The dead of York and Kiev and Warsaw
Lie in no ghetto in the heart.

Our words to mourn them storm the common air
When they are fierce and bleak and fact.

2
From The Proper Blessing

The words that are your daily bread
In me are the dark syllables
Of ~~forgotten~~ prayers.

peace
peace

Poem for My Grandfather

On the Anniversary of his Death

Today, a candle in a glass
Burns slowly on the mantelpiece.
Wheesht, the dead are here.

My father, your grey-haired son,
Tastes again the salt, wax prayers
Of your sacred, dying day.

You are a name, holy in his presence,
The last solemn date
In our calendar of death.

Truly a ghost, my father sees, you.
A kind man's regret softens his face.

But for me there is no introduction:
For me you are a light on the mantelpiece,
A half shadow on the wall.

Yiddish Poet

He moved among blocked facades,
And the remains of an old life kept growing
Here and there, for its quaint satisfaction.
In everything the habit of tragedy
Had framed his saddened view.
Sometimes he could not trust himself to speak
For fear of weeping.

He loved his language
Like a woman he had grown old with,
Whose beauty shone at moments in his memory
But saw how time had stricken what was his
And pondered on the truth of his desire.

And he could not remember his own poems
Yet hoped something would live of them,
The scent perhaps, or a sudden particular cry
Made in a night he summed up suffering.

At the end he wrote always of death
As if it was his meaning all along,
And what he hoped from life was not perfection
But difficult glints of certainty.

For a man was this one intimate with sorrow,
His dreams led nowhere – yet alive he sang.

Isaac

It was my father forced him into the desert –
My father, the patriarch, fearing for my inheritance,
And my mother, jealous of the strength of a concubine's child.

And I vaguely remember the mocking, knowing boy
Who played his secret games around our tents
And crept in at night to his mother the slave woman's pillow.

He could do marvellous things: whistle wild songs,
Climb trees I couldn't, find unknown caves and streams;
His exploits were legend among our lesser household.

But there was that day my father, a man perplexed,
Rejected his furtively proud, unorthodox son:
His God wanted me and my father always listened.

I hear now my brother is chief of a tribe in the desert;
He lives by conquest and has many enemies.
His children plot and starve when he is defeated.

I hear rumours he dreams of marching against me
To seize his inheritance. What shall I do against God and my father?
I, too, believe in the destiny of my children.

I, too, have suffered, perhaps more than he:
I have had a sacrificial knife laid at my throat.
These lands are a small exchange for that terrifying moment.

I would like to help my brother, but he is still proud.
There will be no discussion of peace between us;
And our father, the old God-fearing man, has been dead many years.

'Before There Was...'

'Before there was fighting, the road ran south
Through desert to the sea, but when it ended
The frontier cut across, and we built
Another road across it, for direction
And property had altered.'

The old road lay like a severed arm
Grown used to its lack of blood.

Then we climbed higher round the bends
Of ownership the war had left. He pointed
To a tower the shells had chopped into.
'In that tower a bell hung, and two of our men
Were positioned under it. One shell
Brought the bell down, and they were trapped
And killed below.'

Did he say their bodies, or what was left
Of them, still lay under the wrecked iron,
Or did I not follow his words?

                    At any rate,
For their deaths, a silence passed through us,
All of us held by the sleeping posture of a war.

Before the Trial of Eichmann

The cells of that man's brain are divided among us.
Some have its symbols in blue burned into their arms,
Some have a vacancy they will not ever explore
And others see images of cold, dark shadows
That come screaming after them to beg for a pity
That will never be wholly given.

In all of us the bits of brain cry out, cry
For a whole meaning, cry for a design of the machines
We said were human.

We have found no meaning,
And many fragments we cannot ever recover.

But the brain in us cries, the mind invades our mind,
Crying that we should confront the strange, empty cells.
We should take fragments and give them meaning
For the sake of those who died without meaning.

To us this seems human, to judge
For the sake of those who were denied judgement,

To meet, with the fragments crying in us, a cluster
Of empty cells.

Taste

Often we've sat
With brandy, and drunk in Yiddish
Folk-songs, and talked of the wealth
Of material that must lie buried
In unsearched libraries, in mouldering
Collections.
             I've felt in touch with
Matters of childhood, and thought my broken
Learning redeemed in the wash of origins.

(Why not these songs also?)

But the only record I found
To commemorate those evenings
Played sentimental tunes.
The schmaltz of its arrangements
Fell horribly.

To savour inheritance is not enough.

Jerusalem

The town lies in its warm, blue evening,
I can feel the sleep of its easy stones.
There is a small white moon intoning
Put history by: call in your soul.

The dark, quiet streets, untense and shining,
Rock in their comfortable sounds.
The fury of martyred vision murmurs
Put grieving by: call in your soul,

The passion of these small, bare hills crying
On the last grief of Europe washed in them,
On fabulous, split energies shaping
Put searching by: call in your soul.

Tel Aviv 3.30 AM

At three-thirty there is no-one on the streets
Except a few taxi-drivers lounging in
The settled night.
                                        Just out of sight
The dark sea is bashing its meaningless
Shape against the switched out promenade.

The blocks and blocks of flats and offices
Are smoothly silent.
                                        It is all nearly
As brushed and quiet as in Jerusalem

Though here the moon does not hang
Religiously above the sleeping plaster.

These dense and suddenly set down forms
Are the bright shell an unusual courage
Built, a singular innocence fetched up
On unpromising sand.

                                        It is a city
Like any other now, crowded with commerce,
Dazzled by the glare of brutal public signs.
Its faces shift on fashionable tides.

Yet the name still holds a legend
Peopled by the pride of a rebirth.

There is a quick deft brightness
Lingers on the emptied streets,
And its seventy languages
Merge towards the pacing dawn.

Golders Green Address

The place is bland,
                    trim as any comfortable
Suburb in England,
                    with all the withdrawn look
Of these neat, affluent times,
                         but if you looked closely,
Carefully scrutinized,
                    at times you would see
Small symptoms of alienation
                         among its well-fed residents.
Candles on Friday,
                    a beard or two, an occasional
Joke in Yiddish,
                    but nothing too much,
You understand,
                    to alarm or remind
Of what there is to be alarmed by
Or be remembered.
                         You should not imagine
Anyone in the poised main road
                         would accost
You to blurt out
                    what has come to pass,
And you need hardly fear
                         an over-quizzical look,
Or a misplaced gesture.
                         Though, as I say,
There are one or two signs
                    of otherness.
Still, don't worry.
                    They scarcely jar.

Mr Markson

That old man who came to teach me then
Has blended with many.
                              I can hardly remember now
Just what he looked like,
                              except his black hat,
Yellowish stained beard, and shoulders hunched.
His accent too evades me
                              except that it was broken
Like my grandmother's.

A dark, grey, distant, forgettable man,
Yet three times a week at the dining-room table
He would point to the curling Hebrew script
And pour into me all it said about Creation,
The fall of Adam, and the faith of Abraham.

There was a piety,
                              and something more I couldn't
Understand in all that legend and recital:
A yearning in the old man's broken voice.

Grandmother

Before she died, my grandmother lay all white
In a bed at the far end of a grim ward,
Cut off from the pieties of ninety years.
                                        It was
As though, somehow, the girl she had far away been
Was found again,
                        chattering in Yiddish,
Babbling in a world her orthodoxy kept hidden
All her days.

            Her God tormented her
Till, 'Nem tzu mine neshomme,' she cried – 'Take
Away my soul',
                    but the pain went on,
Exhausting the patience of doctors and nurses
Who could not bear one pious old woman's
Plight,
            who could not know the dignities
Racked in her drab body,
                                or how she was crying.
She died
            through the terrors of a world
That gave no answers
                        to what she cried.

Festa

Today they say was the feast
Of *Corpus Domini*
                    And coming round
By the cathedral, I blundered
Into the vast crowds gathered
To watch the spectacle.
                            There were
Slow drum taps, and then the
Banners came, swaying out of
The great doors, and round the square,
Followed by God's agony carved
On a little cross of sticks.
                            An anthem
Struck up through the well-placed
Loudspeakers, and someone prayed
In a level, finely pitched voice
For the poor, the prisoners, the sick
And unemployed.
                            The crowd answered
Ascoltaci,
            And a white canopy,
Like a *chuppah*, came billowing round.

I saw many near me duck and
Cross themselves in their devotion.

                                    It was
Soaring and death, on the square
Of San Giovanni, a glimpse at a
Beautiful ceremony.
                            I lit a cigarette,
Thoughtfully, and walked away.

Remote Island

There was that lonely island in the North,
Best for the birds, but a few people lived there
In small and difficult crofts.
                              There was a hill
That rose slowly on one side of it, and across the top
Were the ruins of a war-time establishment.
                                        Huge
Water-tanks rusted there, and tough generators
Lay in derelict silence, crumbling.
                              Strong walls had just
A few gaps in them, but broken fences swayed over
The hillside.
              It was like the remains
Of a previous civilisation on the island,
Though it was twenty years or so ago, the place
Was built.
            And strolling through it you could see
How expertly the war had raised it up,
And just as quickly had dismantled it,

Leaving the island, still depopulating,
In its old remoteness, at the edge of things.

Writing

Your last writing covered pages
With huge, thick, sprawling shapes
As though fiercely you were trying to staunch
Some great wound, and as if
Ink were blood.
                    The furious loops
Of the letters tell nothing,
                                except that
Ink or blood was pouring out of you
Over paper that didn't hold.

Travelling Abroad

Documents, scrutinies, barriers,
Everywhere I pass through them,
It seems, without difficulty.
Nothing jars, nothing slips out of place,
Authority is satisfied by my credentials.

Really, it must represent some peak
Of achievement, from a Jewish
Point of view, that is.
                              What a time
It's taken to bring me
To this sort of freedom,
What tolls have been paid
To let me come
                    to this kind
Of passage.
I can appreciate it,
                        believe me,
I can appreciate.

But I find myself wondering,
As I sit at this café table
                              over
A good glass of beer,
Why I don't feel something more
                                    like gratitude,
Why there's some form of acceptance
I don't grasp.

Visiting

It was fine visiting you in Cambridge.
I could see the soft misty elegance
Of that famous town in late November,
And who wouldn't recall a few at least
Of the great names harboured there.
                                    We sat
In a bright hall opposite your college
                              and listened
To an excitingly renowned American poet
Nervously probing his packed, tense lines.
                                    You deserve
All that the place can offer you,
                    all that mysterious learning
In store there.
                I was thinking that, as I walked
Back to the station, between the gentle buildings,
And passed a gang of youngsters, jeering
                              at a Japanese couple.

Where

I find it is Yom Kippur,
                    and here I am
Down by the river
                in late afternoon.
There is a poem
            I have read
In several versions
                about the Jewish writer
Who doesn't fast, who
                    doesn't go to synagogue
On Yom Kippur,
                the day of atonement,
And here is my construction
                        of that poem.
Here am I,
            on the embankment
Staring at the river,
                while the lights
Are coming up,
                signifying darkness, the end of the fast,
Though it's not over yet,
                    and the congregations
Are still gathered
                in the synagogues,
Praying, *slach lonu, m'chal lonu*,
                            forgive us, pardon us,
We have sinned,
                we deserve punishment,
We are like clay
            in the hands of the great Potter,
Who has shaped us all,
                    even, you could say, me
Here by the river,
                watching the water

And the rubbish
                    drifting on the water,
Imagining what is
                    swaying in under the bridges,
Is something of exile,
                    formless but perceptible,
Bringing in the names
                    of pious cities,
Vilna and Minsk and Vitebsk
                    (my own ancestral names)
And vanished communities,
                    behind curtains
Of forgetfulness,
                    and ordinary human change,
Praying communities
                    on Yom Kippur and other days
Clinging to and turning from
                    that which I cling to
And turn from,
                    if you like, the covenant
That keeps me fasting,
                    but not in synagogue
Today, Yom Kippur.
                    I go into the gardens,
Sit down on a bench,
                    read my newspaper
And wait
          for the first star.

Booksellers

It hasn't taken long for even the street to go.
That crowded little street last time I saw it
Was smashed up and naked. Why should I mourn
Except for that bookseller who hoarded his volumes
There in a dark little shop, holy books and profane,
A transient collection brought over from the Continent
When such books were being torn and burnt, by decree?
Huge volumes of Talmud, small volumes of poetry,
Grammar and philosophy, guides for the perplexed,
The fruits of exile carefully reassembled
In another kind of ghetto.
                              After he died, I saw
His shop abandoned, ruined, opened to the illiterate air.
It had suffered a fire, and the burnt, soused collection
Lost touch with its identity.
                              Through the charred mess
I saw a fine copy of the stories of Mendele,
Writer of Yiddish, who called himself 'the Bookseller'.

Sound

In a rough, windy night
I have been listening
To the movements of the wind
And forming a kind of poem
Without knowing its language.

Ruach, I say, using
The old biblical word
For the wind, the breath
Or spirit of God
Moving after creation.

But nothing follows:
No other words
Cross the darkness outside.
There is only *ruach*,
The word for the sound of the wind.

Three Poems about Death

From the Hebrew of Moses Ibn Ezra
Lived and Died in Spain, 11th–12th century

1

A man should remember, from time to time,
That he is occupied with death,
That he is taken a little further
On a journey every day
Though he thinks he is at rest,
Like a ship's passenger lounging on deck,
Being carried on by the wings of the wind.

2

I was stirred to visit the resting place
Of my parents and all my true friends.
I questioned them, but they neither heard
Nor answered me. Have even, I asked,
My own mother and father betrayed me?
Without speaking they called to me
And showed me my own place beside them.

3

There are graves remaining from long ago
In which men sleep out eternity.
There is neither envy nor hatred,
Love nor malice there, and looking
Over them I could not separate
Who was slave and who was master.

Antiquity

It is only an old metal pot
With a half-intelligible Hebrew inscription
Round its middle.
                     No one knows
What it could have been used for.
It was found in an English river
In the seventeenth century.
                         It is medieval,
And stands today in a glass case
In a museum.
                I stare at it,
Wondering.
                Perhaps its message
Is meant for me.

Immigration

I

It wasn't easy getting out of the Tsar's Russia.
They had to bribe and lie.

And it was terrible on the ship.
They couldn't go up deck,
Someone stole all their luggage,
And the children were sick with fever.

Still, she came through it, my young grandmother,
And travelled to Manchester,
Where my grandfather was waiting, with a new language,
In Cheetham Hill.

2

Really, they'd wanted to reach America,
But never saved enough for the tickets,
Or perhaps it was just that their hearts were in the east,
And they could go no further west.

However it was, when Hitler went hunting,
We found that luckily
They had come far enough.

The Hundred Pipers

Dumbfoundered the English they saw, they saw,
Dumbfoundered they heard the blaw, the blaw,
Dumbfoundered they a' ran awa', awa'

I remember how the teacher's voice crowed
As she taught us that song. How we enjoyed it!
I still do, this battle song of my native country.

Looking back,
I wonder what wars she was preparing us for,
That ancient miss.

Return

After a long time in the desert
What is it that brings back poetry
Like water to the Negev?

I don't know. Not virtue
Or debauchery, or any special hardship
Or sudden love.

I'd better, anyhow,
Make the most of it,
And say the proper blessing
For such occasions.

Sol

'See the sun redden towards evening'

Near Malaga, I see the sun
Reddening, yellowing into the blue sea
And think of Shlomo ibn Gabirol,
Malagueñan, who wrote that line.

And this afternoon I drank a cup
Of sweet wine in a hidden square
Where Lorca drank and is remembered,

It is the time of *El Cambio*,
Changing. The Moors are gone,
The Catholic realm is gone,
The heady dictatorships are dregs.

The other end of the Mediterranean,
Where I have also been, fumes.

The poems sing their lusts, their elegies.

Córdoba, Granada, sierras, exile.

Old passions cry in measured times.

Torre del Mar, January 1988

3

From A Bit of Dialect

Speech

Out here in the hills you get
Quite a bit of dialect,

more than many

People would imagine.

It's had a way

Of surviving, breaking out, whatever
Gentility may say,

beyond where education

Leads.

I have an ear for it,

Scots or Yiddish,

raw expression

that

No one's quite sure

how to handle.

Place

'Where do you come from?'
'Glasgow.'
'What part?'
'Vilna.'
'Where the heck's that?'
'A bit east of the Gorbals,
In around the heart.'

Learning

I too was a student of those things,
The texts and commentaries.
My readers know all this,
My references.

And after all that (knowledge buried
Like damaged scrolls of the Torah)
What of it?

It's all asking.
                    Though I've forgotten much
Of the debate and ritual,
The rhythms of learning,
It's still in me to ask and ask.

Breaking

A bad season. War broken out
And round about more personal fears.

In this I am supposed to look
For images, to touch rhythms, to speak.

I have no binding sounds,
No singing linkages,

Can only turn and turn and listen
For some calm to come.

Out

All the poems not collected,
That are left lying in drawers
Among dying papers, or go roaming
On pages one can't recall,
Which of them really exist
And which are imagined?

When sortings take place they glow
And gnaw.

There should be some ceremony
Like *Kol Nidrei*, the solemn cancellation
Of all vows unaccomplished,
For these untended poems.

Whatever one owes them ought
To be erased.

Work

'What do you do?'
'Translate.'
'Oh? What language do you
Translate from?'
'Hebrew.'
A sudden, adjusting silence
And then? And then?

Region

On this side down through the trees
You come to the haugh, and the river
Flowing clearly over its stones.
                                    The field
Across it leads up to the main road,
Duly numbered, signposted and flat.

And on the other side, if you go up
Alongside the burn, into the fields, you come
To a ridge where clumps of heather cling
And you can look down past the curving
Of the hills into the next valley.

                                    Beyond those
More hills bulge up to the sky.
                                    There are
Few buildings, byres mostly, or low cottages
In the distance.
                        On maps it is
All named, this place, accounted for.

But to me looking over it now
Towards the sunset
                        it is a nameless country
That could be mine.

4
'... cold diasporas...'

The poets never lied when they praised
Spring in England.
                    Even in this neat suburb
You can feel there's something to
                    their pastorals.   ~~their pastorals~~

Something gentle, ~~broadly~~, nostalgic, is stirring
The ~~in-drawn bricks~~ and the well-~~kept~~ pavements
On the well-aired pavements.
                            ~~in-drawn brick~~

Sighs and you notice the sudden sharpness
Of things growing.
                    The sun lightens ~~the signif~~
The significance of ~~what the~~ ~~funeral~~
                        ~~what the lines~~
~~Steep in~~   ~~steep in~~
~~Processions~~,
Are steeped in,
                ~~firefly~~s at their
        loosely.
                Early May/touches also/
The cold diasporas that England
                        kindly
                    ~~never~~ mentions.

I Choose Neither ...

I choose neither East nor West,
For I am shaped by the North,
And my history reaches down through old maps
Of Europe, and jumbled alphabets meaning,
'I am for ever. This my Empire stands.'

Only those I seek who say: 'Pain is real,
And not to be put by with a shrug,
Nor exhibited.'
And also: 'Love is more than a gesture' and
'Know what you destroy'.

But those who scrutinize and say:
'You do not fit the pattern of my analysis',
'So many laws are broken here',
'The gods, our teachers, do not like that',
Are those whom I want to avoid, my enemies.

To those who think my choice simple I write:
For these and for want of these
The blood of my relatives and ancestors
Ran down the gutters of empires.

It flows in me like a cold, rough sea.

In Early Spring

Walking in Hampstead in early Spring,
Where the patches of mud on the Heath
Reminded me of Winter's diseases no sun could get at,
I summoned my verses, such as they were,
To survey their afflictions and measure their promise.

And here in this cool English suburb
There grew in me the sound of all the singers
Who turned my people towards Jerusalem,
Or, hopeless in exile, mourned the loss of fulfilment
And the human errors that warped their love.

The Hebrew ones who clung to the purity
Of that vision that promised them return,
Yehudah Halevi, and Moses Ibn Ezra,
A man of love, whose learning served to make
A perfect poem, and know a bad one by instinct;

And afterwards Bialik who came near to seeing
What those ones in Spain knew only was a dream,
Though he knew too what centuries wound round their hearts
Enclosed his people in futility of words,
And rose and sang them out of stupor.

And also those whose sprawling anguish
Spread out in Yiddish across the grim frontiers,
And saw the tongue they nourished dying
Through what they too had longed for.
And those who in the many tongues of Europe

Were figures of exile, voices of victims,
Men torn by what they did not always know.
The ironic Heine, whose sharp sad lyrics,
Removed from the text-books, did not die
But ruined the Germans' perfect solution;

And tragic Rosenberg, whom a war killed
Before he got his great things into words;
My friend Jon Silkin; and those over the Atlantic
Looking at Europe like a distant curse.
And I hear most the miraculous, broken poems

That were made in the enclosures of insanity
Whose authors heard the chanting of the Inquisition
And smelt the smoke of the crematoria
And knew there was no escape, yet wrote
To show how life is at the verges of humanity.

Their great sound grew, and in that company
I walked past the pond and down the hill,
Aware that nothing was ended. With this Spring
They rose to a passionate renewal,
And I must serve their freedoms with my own.

Old Theme

Fathers all, I can meet you
Neither in old ghettos
Nor in newer suburbs
Of diaspora,

Nor even in restored Jerusalem;
But only across the Sambatyon,
That boiling, magic river,
Where the lost tribes live.

Supplication

Lord, from this city I was born in
I cry unto you whom I do not believe in:
(Spinoza and Freud among others saw to that)
Show me in this place in which I started
Where I have gone wrong.

Descend neither in Kirk nor synagogue
Nor university nor pub.

But on a handy summit like Ben Lomond
Make me a new Sinai, and please God
Can we have less of the thou-shalt-not?

Record of a Walk Home

It was a lovely booze-up, and we were
Walking home through the naked midnight streets
Stepping across tramlines like the metal sinews
Of a satisfied city falling into sleep,

When one of us, a medical student, drawled
Of a child as I might speak of a poem
Gone wrong: 'Poor little bastard, got jaundice,
And it's going to die. Nothing to do

But let it.' I stopped sick at the jest
That made a human being serve our drunken
Sentimentality. Then thought: My pity
Orders words to save the growth of life,

But if a car came plunging down this road
And caused an accident, I would stand by
And watch while he fought for the sufferer.

I walked on and caught the others up,
Thinking of either deficiency
That kept our trades apart.

'Out Among...'

Out among the dormitory towns
Of Buckinghamshire we took a wrong turning
And lost our way.
                          We stopped by a signpost
And discovered we were travelling
In a complete circle, without knowing how.
One of the girls made a joke about it
About us outside the ghetto, bewildered
In exile.
                    Only a joke, of course.
                                        The fields
Of the Home Counties at twilight don't
Look that hostile, and we're well provided
With maps.
                    It was just a small diversion,
And we soon hit the right road again

But that moment we stopped was awkward, maybe
More than we said.

N.W.2: Spring

The poets never lied when they praised
Spring in England.
       Even in this neat suburb
You can feel there's something to
           their pastorals.
Something gentle, broadly nostalgic, is stirring
On the well-aired pavements.
          Indrawn brick
Sighs, and you notice the sudden sharpness
Of things growing.
       The sun lightens
The significance of what the houses
Are steeped in,
      brightens out
Their winter brooding.
       Early May
Touches also the cold diasporas
That England hardly mentions.

'Introduction to A Scottish Sequence'

What called me north I do not know
Entirely. Not a piper on a rock
Dirling hypnotic music through my sky,
Nor lust for whisky washed down with strong ale
Against a foggy background of bare hills,
Nor Raeburn's beauties near ethereal
(With jeans and shorter hairstyles, nowadays)
Made me leave her in the south
Who was cool and English, and the fierce
Jewish discussions of unfathomable hate.

I am no exile from a Celtic mist
Nor wanderer from 'the Northern lights
of Aberdeen'. To me exile is a country,
That has the face of the cities of Europe,
A slum face pocked with treacherous suburbs.

And yet looking down South Portland Street
Towards an old fashioned stretch of the River Clyde
I perceive that what I am after is mostly
Again my grandfather, that man strong in Talmud,
(And I myself in Turriff Street long ago
Was taught the dialogue of ingenious rabbis)
What kept him here for almost fifty years,
That calls, but cannot keep me here, for one?
What gave this place the look of an outpost of exile
To woo the east here in his daily prayers?

His son's son, I cross the river into town
Looking for bejeaned models of Raeburn (or any
Other painter) or listening to neutral music.

The old man's secret rests with him
Behind these stricken stones.

Poem

I am a tall talmudic Jew
With a slightly Scots accent.
You are English whom the sun
Never tans, but strokes your white skin.
Between us we lay bare your breasts
And gently my fingers pluck and gently
Your arms enfold.
               Where afterwards
Sad colours in the sky grow from
I do not know.

A Joke Across the North Sea

Watching the neat, vacant firth
Opposite the dull shoulder of Fife coast
I stood at the edge of the sea's doorstep.

One of an island bundle, I heard
The poet Heine calling to Scotland
Across the cold, liberating waves.

Ha, how you would laugh, dead sweet-bitter singer,
To hear one, tugged like you, at the seams of his Jewish coat,
Rise, like me, to try and answer.

'My Fathers Planned Me...'

My fathers planned me with their prayers
And gave me their coded, ancient learning.
I heard their urgent voices where I walked,

But took my love in my arms
And found a human music in her voice
And named as joy what they explored with law.

We are a new people, she and I,
Whose lilts are pagan and have no appointed sound.
Away and far down my ghosts whisper a weak song.

January Poem

Snow, Joan, has captured the garden
And frozen up its customary look.
A white witch's waste crawls from the window
Towards pure vertices of light,

While unsung silence menaces all thought –
The black masked window passes it inside;
Our piled communities are split to fiery bits
By the whitefall artist's slicing midnight grasp.

In this I write to tell you how the warmth
Of your whole being melts surrendered space,
Who are a glowing island in mysterious snow,
A source of sound in long regions of silence.

Mosaic

Her craft is to fit stones
To make a bird, a prophet,
A huge face examined
By its cracks.

Of ways of making
This would seem most painful,
Stone by bit of coloured stone.

At distance the labour is concealed,
But draw near and something
Of the process talks up violently
In small squares that fight against
Their rhythms.

Which one of us could bear
Such naked art,
Who tick down and smooth
The flow of words
Lest our flaws cry out
In the terrible gaps of speech.

We stand in quarries
Where the stones come brittle
And the colours blear.

'In an East Coast Fishing Village'

In an east coast fishing village
I sat on a brown rock and watched
Four women lift their skirts
And wade into the sea.
Their legs gleamed white in the salt air,
Moving against the reiterated squeal of a gull,
And the clean retch of tide on the crisp sand.
In that slow silent procession
I saw across the empty beach
Four figures enter the legendary landscape
Of song bound kings, and ballad princesses.
Easily, easily in this land a little distance
Transforms the living and the dead into kingdoms
Of romance and wild splendour –
Even the blackest squalor of the foulest slums.

'Lately...'

Lately up in the Lake District
I took a walk from Keswick
To see the famous cataract
                              of Lodore
Well, now the guidebook admits
The poet exaggerated.
                                        Where was
That stirring flow of water I've always

Wanted to witness since the words first
Cascaded through my classroom?
                                                    I saw
Only a narrow strip of water, making
No great commotion.
                              And all poets, I thought,
(As others have found) exaggerate, or worse,
And who does it matter to?

So Always

So always a dark past surrounds me
With its figures broken across strange tongues
And places unreconciled. I am moved
By what I cannot fathom, hurt by what
I cannot hold.
                    Yet it is no mere theme
Of unresolved longing I follow in the shifting
Trappings of my verse.
                              It is no lost look
At a fabulous kingdom I hunt down.

                              What I hold after is an
Image of the sad, piercing lyric, the mighty
Beaten faith that fires my blood,

                    That was never yet gathered,
Trim and labelled, in the courts of style.

5
'... to my Promised Land'

נסיתי לכתוב על החיים של בֶּבֶּל

בַּעֲבָר אֶזכּוֹר, אֲני וַהֶבְרֶר

אבל בשם בו אך ב אולן

גוֹאֵל אֵיק זה היה, וְאֵיך הִיכָּשֵל,

Notes for Uriel Da Costa

b. Oporto c. 1590 – d. 1640, Amsterdam

Before adolescence I discovered you.
Now I can hardly recall the soulless terrors
Your tragedy gave
Me, the violence of your
Heresies,

      pitching through my childhood's
Talmud Torah.
          Your fevers to believe,
Return and believe, grasped me
And pleaded for a pity I could never
Have defined.
         Disgraced in the synagogue,
Excommunicated, I could shiver
At your drama,
        your suicide seemed
An infinite passion.

        But I have come now
Through books and books on laws and suffering,
And you are banished to a couple of pages
In Graetz's 'History'.
        If I could, though,
I'd trace you out,
        call up your anguish
That stalked the small scholar I was,
Recover what burned and moved me in your fate.

Dr Zamenhof

The inventor of Esperanto

I remember you also,
Who in Warsaw constructed words
You hoped we'd take, clean
Of the scratching, smeared connotations
We grow weird in
To speak with the heart of international man
The lonely accumulations
Of misheard humanity.

Ni ne parolas la Esperanton,
And you remain a high-thinking scholar
Who sketched a fragile, impossible dream
Over the impassioned wars of our condition
A kind of poor joke on our becultured selves.

You died, I think, before you could have seen
That makers of sound world language must provide
For the curious love of Yiddish and German
On the fields of Auschwitz.

Patterns of Culture

Behind the wire, unadorned with strangeness,
Was an ordinary pigeon,
The like of which has the freedom
Of Trafalgar Square.

Yet there among the poor rarities
Of the Belgrade Zoo
He was alien, therefore kept
On display out

Of the common air. 'But in London …'
I reacted. No-one stirred.
Between me and the dull grey pigeon
Were the habits of Yugoslavia.

On a Balkan Visa

In the south of that country I passed
Through a poverty I had never seen,
Where the people moved in postures
Of childishness, you could not even call
Despair.
              This was a peasanthood
That stood not hard against its land,
But slid and shuffled over it
With an empty look.
                    The importance
Of men who sat before boxes on which
They scrubbed their strength into other
People's shoes. The huddled bundles
In railway stations, that did not know
How to look or stand with human purpose.
The smell and decay of those below
Minimal significance.
                    Over this was
Cried Democracy, the People had been
Told of their own sovereignty.
                              Of compassion
No-one had told them, or explained
How they lay far below the beginning
Of such words.
              They had not even
The sharp hurts of children.

'Behind the Synagogue...'

Behind the synagogue was a small room
A place obviously to study in
With a high chair at one end of it

'This (they said) was Rashi's college. Here
The great commentator is supposed to have taught.'
But no-one knows if it was really true
More likely it was just a legend, and Rashi
Never even was in Worms.
                      Though there were
Other Jews living here, till the Nazis came
And destroyed them and
               all the synagogues.

And then, of course, the Nazis were destroyed
And the new democracy of Germany rebuilt
The synagogue and the legendary room of Rashi
Exactly as it was before.
              So the myth
Was recreated.

Woman Figure, South Turkey

At hip height,
With wooden blocks held out for legs,
You occupy the pavement;
And as I meet your expression,
Arranged with silly sly hope among your fossiled limbs
I can't take what it expatiates about the
Human condition.

What shall I place between your lack and mine?

A shrewd determinist, the tourist knows the facts
Of economic conditions etc.,
And should be calm and objective,
(After all *I* don't live here)
Pass you a coin and remember you
Are part of the scenery.

What shall I place between your lack and mine?

In a spasm of fear I turn away
To cry down the men playing cards
Under the beautiful trees –
The harbour too is very beautiful –
And the draggle of filth
That overspreads my reason.

What shall I place between your lack and mine?

Down through those streets
A little way out on the blue water
There is a boat that goes a two days' journey
To my promised land.
I have no money left
To hold towards you.

What shall I place between your lack and mine?

In repeated visions some
Have seen even you comforted,
Taken into the arms of whatever
Monstrous god could mend
Your sores.
I can't get down to where love
Begins in you.
I can't
Easily pass you.

What shall I place between your lack and mine?

Menorah

The symbol of this land is a seven branched
Candelabrum pressed up against the sun.

They ask me, the glowing ones, here,
'Does your heart hold up its fingers

Hard and alight, like our bare symbol?'
'My hand burns, here, my hand burns.'

Bab El Wad

Limbs of trucks, hallowed
By a fierce sacredness,
Among the rocks of this gorge
Where in the small war
They were smashed
Lie in savage eloquence

In a dialect that disowns
Hillsides laid with trees,
Heavy with the spirit
Of European martyrdoms.

Bare iron driven on rock
Proclaims a posture of dying
That is of this land,
And it only.

Raw and sacred, death
Is proclaimed that we,
Inlaid with other death,
Are strange to.

Lesson of History

In my room at the crumbling edge
Of Jerusalem, I read far into the night
On the beginning of English history.

The invasions of Iberian, Celt,
Angle, Dane, Saxon, Norman and others
Forgotten, who swooped on the forests

And heath of that untracked island
Named it, and worked out a language
Suddenly shift out of lists I learned

At school. When the writer says 'horde'
I think I can see men descending from ships
Mounting the beaches and travelling inland.

When he says 'village', I think I feel
A collection of huts, men working the fields,
And a lord demanding and owning their labour.

Quaint dead customs, titles, loyalties
Spawn and settle out of chaos
I see the choices history confirms.

The sky, outside the cave of my room,
Is very clear. The stars can be told
By amateur astronomers.

Under the clear image of the sky, I wonder,
What forms breed here? What language grows?
Whose choice or action will endure

And shape the histories with schooled clichés?
If that comes will they be redeemed
More easily than in England – now?

Israeli Arab

His English was smooth and graceful,
And his Hebrew better than mine
Will ever be. He talked charmingly
Of Nazareth his home town
And its centuries-old, strange customs.
But his gift for holding together
Politeness in several cultures concealed
An injury, and his voice turned
Attention to itself, by reaching
Towards tones we need never seek.
He was trying, of course, to make
The best of an impossible situation.
Meeting him that evening I was mostly silent,
Though I have access to three or four cultures, myself.

Painter

We talked of Chagall tonight,
His curved red cow
That almost winks at you,
His lovers planted side by side
In the thick bouquets
Of the dancing villages
Of hard hasidic joy.

Walking home, I couldn't help it,
The moon sailed on a fiddle
In the sky. The traffic-lights
Danced green circles over the roofs.
From my feet the ground
Ran into poems the colour
Of this man's fervent world.

And my arms summoned
The climbing lilters of the streets
To a waved Sabbath, fresh as a new calf.

Sabbath Morning: Mea Shearim

They came along the street, with huge fur hats,
Discussing, the soft bulks of prayer shawls
In their arms, or with the woollen maleness of shawls
Wrapped as holy armour round their backs,
And I was nearly seeing them as long ago, when
In the cold, wide synagogues I laid my shawl
And dreamed this way I would become a man.

Religious Quarter

Grandfather, today I walked in Mea Shearim
And it was a little like it must have been
In Vilna seventy years ago.

                          Small boys
Walked between their dangling curls
With already the strange sensuality of Talmud
Scholars. Merchants, in fur hats, relaxed
In the slow pace of their closed, coinless
Sabbath: matrons went with their love blown
Away into a nagging over-all welfare
And young girls were concealing their sex
In a terrible kind of shapelessness.

                              And all this
Under the hot sky of Jerusalem.

It was a little, grandfather, of the sea
Of the past, out of which you sailed
To leave me in the north,

                         whose speech
I take to tame, oh, centuries of such
Isolated quarters striving in my blood.

Hills

A wind grinding slow and fine
Over the black road. To my left
Clusters of light across the dark stones,
And on the right a high enclosure
Of military graves.
                 An eerie moment:
This is the country where miracles
Were in repute. An extraordinary
Flash met travellers on roads like this,
Blinding revelations disturbed the universe.

                 The moment passes.
I walk on in a restored darkness,
The road stretches where it has to.
Stones crunch firm-edged under my feet.

The stars stay shining apart, though,
Distant, given to mystery.

Lesson Number 24

This is a country where guns are known.
Not apparatus of pageantry,
But carried to use at the sudden edge
When suspicion lets its dogs leap free.

I shiver at them laid on a café table
Or one on a shoulder in the street.
Where I was born, in that careful island,
A gun was never a thing you could meet.

Here where the sky is clear and sharp
They're handled with exactitude.
Addressed with a sort of unprobed passion,
Can be the quick agents of a mood.

The Departure

At sunrise we sighted his departure
Halfway up the hillside
And though we knew he would go
Into his own oblivion
As if we had not driven him
Our souls called him back;
But he was among the morning cries
Of the indifferent birds, and the rocks
Moved him into a familiar background.

This scene requires belief
Though not as he demanded
With a cry to the soul and a promise.
We remain among his burning words.

His words burned in the shadow of our existence
As the truth burned in his brain:
All the elements sufficed to wield his truth
Yet the tools were easily divided.

To fashion images of truth
He chose the future, and arranged its scenes
With a single meaning. There was no
Gap a poet leaves.

All this we understand
Though we rejected him.
It is bitter in a corner of our hearts.

Perhaps I should have gathered my doubts
Into an echoing call of return.
Would the city drag my voice
Down from the revealing wind?

It is too late now.
The gods of the city call for worship

And he is gone into his own oblivion.

Over There, Just Here

From the observation post you can see them.
'It is quite safe', my friend says, 'only,
Do not point.
                    This barbed wire here
Is the frontier: that house just there belongs to them.
Sometimes you see a car jolt down that road.
It's an odd feeling.

Night-time their shadows light up with ours,
Go to bed with ours.
It's an odd feeling.

There has been no trouble now for four years.
Things have settled down to this unruffledness.
But don't point.'

By Kiryat Shemona

It was these hills in the beginning
Baked with fine purple and shaped
With sored cheeks of rock hacked out.
It was trails over these hills, the first
Forms.

      Later is lost among codes
And poetry. What came down
To a significant wandering
In the desert, to an eventual
Sky of massacre is sunk
Beyond the cleverest probing.

      But in the beginning,
Clearly and beyond speech, there were
These hills.

Afterwards

Last night there were two jackals
Crying outside my door.
At first I did not recognise their pitiful sound,
Thinking it was human,
But by the way it hovered on the edge
Of the classes of pain
I placed it among the animal hills
Where I make no sense.

Afterwards, in the removal of their strange sound,
I could feel your cry,
That came against me without name
Or meaning I could place,
Except that your grief split this town
From end to end.
Tell me, did I tame it wrongly, now it has
Entered into words?

To a Teacher of Hebrew Literature

You have no shame, you pronounce,
Like the shame of us who cling
To what, after all, we are:
Split at the foot of several cultures
And approved by none.

You are immensely satisfied to be where you are
And to have what you have.
No-one can touch you.

God, girl, your Israel is a ghetto
Narrower and more firmly surrounded
Than any we have known.
Its walls are built from an academic vision
Of a thing you have never felt.

Child, bone of my bone, flesh of my flesh,
When you speak of normality, of shame
Of cowardice, and of
The human ridge where we find being,
You play with things you do not understand.

Report

Suddenly, I read in a newspaper
About an Arab poet,
Whose name I've never heard of,
Whose work I don't know,
In the land of Israel, in Palestine,
Fined, suppressed, threatened with imprisonment
For 'incitement',
And I want to shout:
Let his poetry survive in its valley
Making nothing happen,
Let him demonstrate his types of ambiguity,
Let him speak awkwardly, inadequately,
Like the rest of us,
For himself.

6
'Place'

There was always journey upon journey,
~~The heart divided~~
My father's, and his father's, and beyond
I can think only of ~~restless~~ men, ~~who~~ who
~~Who~~ ~~lived~~ lived in the ~~continual~~ ~~of this~~ undertaking

~~Say~~ I cannot say ~~as~~ that one emerging day
~~I turned, and freed~~
Their uncompletion was a kind of love,
~~To say there the Name my ~~father~~~~
That ~~so long~~ the Name ~~could~~ ~~may~~ grow ~~even a little~~
For the Name was always human,
Spoke of needs,
~~By~~ their going the Name would grow
That going would make the Name grow,
For ~~the~~ ~~Name~~ was human, spoke of need
Their ~~following~~ the Name towards the four
Unknown corners of the earth was growth
For the Name was human, ~~must~~ be

About Making

It is as well to be careful,
To pare down statement,
To keep close
To the unsayable.

But also to bear in mind
There is deliberate silencing,
To speak up against it
To make oneself heard.

'All Poets...'

All poets are Jews,
Tsvetaeva said.

When the fury and spite
Of the loudly virtuous
Build up around me
(Oh it happens, I assure you)
I can't always tell
Whether it's the Jew in me
Or the poet
They've got their sights on.

Hatred, anyway, is hatred
And always comes
To the same thing.

Leeds Pub

The little hunchback at the microphone
Paused when her croon broke down
To laugh 'O, hell!' at her listeners,
And a young man, tall and husky,
Intoned 'High Noon' with true humility.

My poems lay in a folder flung
Among glasses on the rough table,
And I ached to join the passionate
Procession of singers beside the pianist
Giving out their deep desire for expression;

But though their songs were feebly turned
And wrong, mine were forged for conflicts
They would not comprehend.
At closing time, going up the cobbled street
A wordless singing filled my head.

Tongue

It can come lowpin' up in me an' a',
This wey o' talkin'.
I dinnae ken whit tae dae wi' it
But it's there richt eneuch.

Dear Mr Leonard

I wonder whether you'd be
Interested,
But one Saturday afternoon
During the course of a religious discussion
An aunt of mine remarked to me:
'Ah'm no froom
Bit whan Ah see them
Ee'in the trayfi meat
It scunners me.'
I found this very striking
And it occurs to me
You could use it
In one of your poems.
Anyway, you might want to
Think about it.

'It's as Though Someone Took an Axe'

It's as though someone took an axe
To my writing desk

My work's chopped up, scattered

Much lost.

After this savaging, what is there
To find among the damage?

'Despite the Real Spite'

Despite the real spite
And making nothing happen
What is it that survives?

Rhythm imperfectly recognised
A feeling for words
Craftily organised,
Emotion collected with fragility.

And what is the reaction?
Too little recognition or too much
Of a wrong kind.

Despite the real spite,
Continue.

Something may penetrate,
Something inaudible otherwise
May be heard.

The Skuas

(For Pirjo)

It hardly seemed believable
                        that those birds
Would come for us,
                but they did, swooping
Into our faces,
                  then up, turning and steadying
On black and white wings,
                        aiming, and down again
There was a war between us
                  and the taut
                            intelligences
We stood still and fascinated,
                    intruders, exposed.

'From Oban...'

From Oban the islands drift away
Into the Gaelic West
                    They're out there now
Beyond the bay,
                    with all their dying
Culture
          rubbed out
                    almost past
The point of revival.
                    There's not much left
To sail in, across the blue waters
Of the Hebrides.

'Back in Manchester...'

Back in Manchester, after a long time,
I saw the streets where the Jews used to live
Are derelict, disappearing.

That unwalled ghetto is being
Transported, dispersed
Into some kind of elegance.

And Whitechapel, too, is being made over
New roads and tall blocks
Cut across old clusterings
Of aspiration.

The Gorbals, it's said, is rising
In skyscrapers.

Why should I not celebrate
Such rehousing,
Such furthering of diaspora?

'Among These Green Hills'

Among these green hills
And weaving lanes
Clear sunsets
Bring back Jerusalem
And I don't know
Whether it is earthly Jerusalem
Under whose walls
I lived for three years long ago
Or some earlier Jerusalem
Whose vision moved me
In this country
Longer ago.

What Are You Talking About?

Afterwards, as we know,
There are those who virtuously
Declare: We didn't know.

Things happened somewhere else,
Or didn't happen like that,
Or we weren't really told.

Anyway, we had no power
To alter or divert
What did or didn't go on.

It's a familiar sound
To be heard among us now,
The deceiving whine of those
Who participate and know.

Hitching

We used to curse all the cars
That calmly passed us by
As we waited often
In unrelenting weather.

But those that didn't stop
Were right,
After all.

We weren't going anywhere,
Together,
You and I.

Edinburgh New Town

In Heriot Row, on a misty November evening
When the lamps were lit early in the cold damp,
We passed the house of Stevenson, and found
A metal plaque outside with a stanza of the poem
About Leerie we both knew.
                              We were glad
To remember that 'Child's Garden of Verses'
It came from, glad to remember the way
It was read to us, or we read it, long ago.

A most Stevensonian evening (was it not?)
As we walked along the pavement of that fine terrace,

Back through our childhoods, in those suburbs
That brought us together, and drove us apart.

State

Here in my native country
I'm answering for somewhere else.

Exile within exile.
Who's a Jew? Who's a Scot?

What happens after independence?

How much history does anyone need?

What's worth fighting for?

Banal questions posed over and over.

This year in Jerusalem, next year in Edinburgh,
Self –?

A CALL TO

GREATNESS

Challenging
Our Next President

DAVID M. ABSHIRE

ROWMAN & LITTLEFIELD PUBLISHERS, INC.
Lanham • Boulder • New York • Toronto • Plymouth, UK

ROWMAN & LITTLEFIELD PUBLISHERS, INC.

Published in the United States of America
by Rowman & Littlefield Publishers, Inc.
A wholly owned subsidiary of The Rowman & Littlefield Publishing Group, Inc.
4501 Forbes Boulevard, Suite 200, Lanham, Maryland 20706
www.rowmanlittlefield.com

Estover Road
Plymouth PL6 7PY
United Kingdom

Distributed by National Book Network

British Library Cataloguing in Publication Information Available

Library of Congress Cataloging-in-Publication Data

Abshire, David M.
    A call to greatness : challenging our next president / David M. Abshire.
        p. cm.
    Includes bibliographical references and index.
    ISBN-13: 978-0-7425-6245-5 (cloth : alk. paper)
    ISBN-10: 0-7425-6245-X (cloth : alk. paper)
    1. Presidents—United States. 2. Political leadership—United States.
I. Title.
JK516.A37 2007
352.230973—dc22   2007041460

Printed in the United States of America

⊗™ The paper used in this publication meets the minimum requirements of
American National Standard for Information Sciences—Permanence of Paper
for Printed Library Materials, ANSI/NISO Z39.48-1992.

CONTENTS

INTRODUCTION

AMERICA TODAY faces profound challenges at home and abroad. Taken together, they constitute nothing less than a "gathering storm," the likes of which our nation has not seen in many years. In order to meet these challenges effectively, the next President will need to unite the nation as it has been united in its finest moments—such as the Revolution and World War II—and both devise and carry out a grand strategy for American renewal. It is easy for candidates and Presidents to talk a good line on national unity, but, for the man or woman elected in 2008, restoring this critical source of American strength will be a requirement.

I strongly agree with the frank but wise account of national challenges, Presidential history, and strategic recommendations presented in the pages that follow. David Abshire, a lifelong public servant, has been an advisor to Presidents, an Assistant Secretary of State, an Ambassador to NATO, a founder of the Center for Strategic and International Studies and now heads the Center for the Study of the Presidency. Here, he draws on his own experience as well as his impressive knowledge of past Presidential successes and failures to present an indispensable guide to Executive Office leadership and a roadmap to restoring America's financial freedom, unity of action, and position in the world. David can be a critical judge, and his recommendations may not jibe with the conventional wisdom of campaign politics—but his concept of civility and strategic vision needs to be heard in 2008 more than ever. As the polls tell us, the American public has had enough. They yearn for accountability and competence in both the Executive and Legislative branches.

David Abshire and I came to Washington over four decades ago from very different backgrounds. A West Point graduate who served in Korea, David finished his Ph.D. in History from Georgetown University in 1959, and shortly thereafter became director of the House Republican Policy Committee. I came as a Senate staffer for Hubert Humphrey in 1949. We both witnessed the Cuban Missile Crisis and worked together to overcome the second missile crisis of the mid-1980s. In those years the Soviets were making their final attempt to break the backbone of the transatlantic alliance through deploying SS-20 missiles. David was then our Ambassador to NATO, rallying our allies against the Soviets, while I was the strategic arms negotiator in Geneva, frequently visiting him at NATO head-quarters for our reports. As special counselors to the President we were fortunate to have been involved in the successful man-agement of a near-disaster. In both of these missile crises—in 1962 and in the 1980s—the nation and our allies were unified in our strategic goals, and mobilized to respond decisively. If there had been divisions abroad and polarization at home, we would have lost the Cold War, as we seem to be losing our global stature today. The adage for this book is, appropriately, Lincoln's: "A House Divided Against Itself Cannot Stand."

In Part I, David offers a tour de force of Presidential his-tory and distills seven characteristics essential to leadership in the highest office. He somberly notes that one or two of these qualities will not be enough. Early in his Senatorial career, John Kennedy, and more recently Michael Beschloss, artfully and powerfully explored the quality of courage. But courage alone is insufficient, and blind courage can be dangerous. If "courage" leads a President to become isolated from potential allies and advisors—if it means retreating into the "White House Bubble," which, as David shows, has brought tragedy to numerous Presidents—then courage ceases to be a virtue. Particularly in a time of war, courage must be leavened with trust. When Presidents have lost trust, we have tended to lose wars.

This book differs from more conventional studies in stressing the power of building coalitions and partners. Both David and I were close to the late professor Richard Neustadt, arguably the "Dean" of Presidential historians, who tirelessly advocated the power of persuasion as a Presidential tool. In this book, David focuses on the power of persuasion in forging alliances and partnerships with Congress and with the private sector as well. Indeed, David effectively demonstrates that unity and civility are not just good-sounding ideals but tools of power in their own right. Too often Presidents have ignored this insight.

We should note and applaud the last section of this book, which calls for the next President to be a grand strategist. The two model Presidential grand strategists are particularly well-chosen. The first, Abraham Lincoln, was a near genius. We may despair if we conclude, with no disrespect to the candidates, that there does not appear to be a Lincoln in sight. The second example is Franklin Roosevelt, who was neither a genius nor a great manager, but a superlative leader. Between them, they elucidate six critical components of effective grand strategy.

Roosevelt knew his weaknesses—he could be impatient and lacked a grasp of detail—and this is what allowed him to so ingeniously organize effort and enlist talent during the Depression and World War II. He also knew how to reach out. A year and a half before Pearl Harbor, the formerly partisan

New Deal leader ended his partisanship and started to include talented Republicans in his efforts for victory. This is just one of the lessons from this book with which I strongly agree. If the next President wishes to answer the call to greatness, this is an indispensable guide.

August 1, 2007
Max M. Kampelman*
Vice Chairman
Board of Trustees
Center for the Study of the Presidency

---

* Max M. Kampelman was from 1980 to 1983 Ambassador to the Conference for Security and Cooperation in Europe; from 1985 to 1989 Ambassador and Head of the United States Delegation to the Negotiations with the Soviet Union on Nuclear and Space Arms in Geneva; and from 1987 to 1989 Counselor of the Department of State. He then rejoined the law firm of Fried, Frank, Harris, Shriver, and Jacobson, LL.P.

Ambassador Kampelman serves as Chairman Emeritus of the American Academy of Diplomacy, Georgetown University's Institute for the Study of Diplomacy, the Woodrow Wilson International Center for Scholars, and Freedom House.

In 1999, President Bill Clinton awarded him the Presidential Medal of Freedom, the nation's highest civilian award. In 1989, President Reagan awarded him the Presidential Citizens Medal, which recognizes "citizens of the United States who have performed exemplary deeds of service for their country or their fellow citizens."

FOREWORD

A NDY GROVE, legendary cofounder of Intel, has written about moments when corporations reach "strategic inflection points." Once in a while, argues Grove, the external environment changes so much that a company cannot continue doing business as usual. Either it must courageously forge a new path and is able to rise, or it is unable to break old patterns and sinks. Is it not increasingly apparent that the United States has reached its own strategic inflection point?

That is why the next Presidency of the country may be the most fateful in decades. Indeed, it is arguably true that no chief executive will have faced challenges of greater consequence and intractability since Franklin Roosevelt took office in 1933. With success, as with FDR, the nation could once again blaze an upward path, but with failure, the United States could accelerate a long slide from greatness—at a perilous price for itself and the world at large.

In these pages, David Abshire captures well the nature of the challenges ahead and provides invaluable counsel for the incoming President and his or her team. Writing in the tradition of Richard Neustadt, whose memos were so helpful to an incoming John Kennedy, Ronald Reagan, and Bill Clinton, Abshire brings history alive, drawing from it wise lessons for the President immediately upon taking office. Mark this down for required reading in the next White House.

Yet Abshire would be the first to recognize that the success of the first hundred days in office also depends heavily upon the hundred days *before* inauguration. It's the preparation for leadership that can make or break a presidency as much as the exercise of power once in office. Before turning to the larger lessons of this book, then, it is worth reflecting for a moment upon the run-up to January 2009. Three goals seem especially important in today's context.

First, the next president should work right now—during the campaign—to secure a clear mandate when voters go to the polls in November 2008. Experience has repeatedly shown that those candidates who not only win the election but also receive a mandate from the people can achieve far more once in office. FDR swept into Washington with a resounding mandate for change and soon swept Congress with him. In the campaign of 1952, Dwight Eisenhower promised to "go to Korea," and the support he thus gained enabled him to end an unpopular war without first achieving military victory. LBJ vowed to build a Great Society in the campaign of 1964, securing popular support for a blizzard of social legislation in the years that followed. And every senescent voter who went to the polls in November 1980 knew that Reagan was promising to cut taxes, cut spending, cut regulation, and boost defense and balance the budget; a Democratic Congress soon went along with him. Contrast that with the early, struggling days of Presidents who didn't seek a mandate—from Kennedy and Nixon to the two Bushes and Clinton. Mandates matter.

Candidates in the 2008 election clearly face a dilemma. If they tell the truth to voters about the tough choices ahead—on national security, health care, entitlement reform, climate change, public education, and more—they risk losing their chances for victory. No politician these days likes to talk about sacrifice or higher taxes. But if a candidate wins by ducking the hard questions, it will be nearly impossible to govern successfully. Voters don't trust Presidents who bait and switch. What to do? Given the magnitude and urgency of the choices ahead, surely the best advice is revealed within history: our best Presidents have been those who have taken prudent but courageous risks.

Second, the next President should be spending time reading not only Abshire and Neustadt but also the classic by Stephen Hess, *Organizing the Presidency*. We think of our Presidents making lonely decisions in the Oval Office. Remember the haunting picture of JFK, standing by himself, bowed, deep in reflection? Certainly there are moments when the President and the President alone must decide. But the best Presidents have always been those who assembled and led the best teams—witness Washington and Lincoln in particular. And in government today—just as in corporations—the quality of the men and women serving a President is more vital than ever.

To our discredit as a nation, we have allowed the appointments process for the Executive branch to break down. In Kennedy's time, an average of two and a half months passed between the time of a Presidential nomination and Congressional confirmation; that span has widened decade after decade so that under Clinton, it reached eight and a half months, and under George W. Bush, no less than nine months. An incoming President may be ready on day one to bark out orders but little will happen because his departments are mere shells. Congress and the Executive branch should long ago have cleared away the bureaucratic obstacles and streamlined the appointments process.

With reform still over the horizon, the Presidential nominee of each political party should act now—before the election—to begin quietly assembling names for potential appointments throughout the Executive branch. Reagan appointed a top-flight New York headhunter, Pen James, to conduct such a process; the morning after the President-elect announced a cabinet nominee, James was there at the doorstep with a notebook full of names and resumes for the nominee to consider. As a result, Reagan got off to one of the fastest, most effective starts in years.

In this cycle, it will also be important for the President-elect to ensure a wide diversity of talent in supporting roles. Coming off more than a decade of poisonous polarization in Washington and given the tough choices ahead, a new President must be a master at consensus building. There is no better place to start than in appointments. At a time of national peril, as Doris Kearns Goodwin has written, Lincoln carefully assembled a "team of rivals"; so did Churchill in May 1940.

Finally, the winner in November should not wait for Inaugural Day but should seize upon the transition to set the tone and thrust of the next Presidency. History shows that the quality of a transition can change the political landscape, deepening popular support for a President in the crucial, early months of governing or—if badly done—introducing a sense of buyers' remorse. FDR, Ike, Kennedy, and Reagan also ran excellent transitions and could hit the ground running once in office; by contrast, the teams around Jimmy Carter and Clinton rue to this day opportunities squandered during their transitions.

Setting the tone does not mean that the President-elect should start issuing policy pronouncements. FDR craftily eluded Herbert Hoover's attempts to draw him into policy-making during the transition, and historians agree that he was smart to do so. FDR knew that the country can have only one President at a time and by holding his cards close, he built up public anticipation for his arrival. What "setting the tone" means can be illustrated by Reagan during his transition: he periodically came to Washington and reached out in highly symbolic ways to leaders in both parties, to leaders of the press (starting with Katherine Graham), and to people on the streets. He showed that he wasn't going to treat Washington as an alien place but as his new home and that he and Nancy would be friendly, new neighbors. He put a smile on his presidency long before he moved in.

Consensus building in today's politics may sound like a hopeless dream. We have been fiercely divided for a decade and a half. But the American people seem to sense that serious danger is now lurking about us, and that is when we have traditionally rallied as a people. A President who appeals to what Lincoln called "the better angels in our nature"—who asks for a courageous mandate, who builds a ministry of talents, and governs on behalf of all of the people—is the President who can lead us once again to the lofty heights.

September 1, 2007
David Gergen
Professor of Public Service
Director, Center for Public Leadership
Harvard's Kennedy School
Center for the Study of the President, Trustee

PART I

"A House Divided Against Itself Cannot Stand"

ABRAHAM LINCOLN, 1858

CHAPTER 1

THE GATHERING STORM

A STORM IS gathering, threatening the celebrations that will surround the inauguration of the President-elect on January 20, 2009. Already, we have begun to see the erosion of America's strategic and financial freedom, the hollowing of its military, and the faltering of its ability to create and lead meaningful alliances. Worse may yet come. The President will inherit a polarized nation and a host of profound challenges at home and abroad. The clouds have been forming for many years; the rain has begun. But deluge is not inevitable. This is no natural storm; it is a creation of man—and man has the power to ward it off. The time for action is now.

When the new President takes office, he or she will face the task of running a country that is the strongest in the world, but, paradoxically, a vulnerable one. There is much good news. We have high productivity, low inflation, and strong economic growth. We produce almost one third of global economic output and own 40 percent of global stock market capitalization. Eighteen of the top twenty universities worldwide are on American soil, and we have led a worldwide

> ∾ **The next President will face the task of running a country that is the strongest in the world, and paradoxically, the most vulnerable.**

information revolution. We remain a country of promise and opportunity to people throughout the world. We are a nation of resilient and optimistic people who have come from every corner of the globe. We have faced great adversity before, and we have prevailed.

Yet, the challenges today are daunting. The war in Iraq is only the most obvious—and the most pressing—issue that will face the new President. He or she will assume command of an unfinished mission in Afghanistan and Iraq, a bellicose Iran intent on acquiring nuclear weapons, and restive populations from Cairo to Kashmir. Russia and China—though not formally our enemies—continue to assert their independence from American might. Some say that America has lost its ability to bring out the better natures of people across the world. That is not all. With Islamic fundamentalism on the rise, the threat of another devastating terrorist attack on our homeland remains high. Battered but not beaten in Afghanistan, al-Qaeda has regrouped in the mountains of northwest Pakistan.[1]

At home, the financial security of the next generation is imperiled by our addiction to debt, easy credit, the likely insolvency of Social Security, and runaway healthcare costs, which afflicts all citizens and drives many businesses overseas. Politicians in both parties remain timid in the face of these potential catastrophes.* We are overly dependent on foreign oil, and face the long-term challenge of costly adaptations to climate change. Globalization and the information revolution have

---

* Only the current Comptroller General, David M. Walker, fully sounds the alarm. With his fifteen-year appointment, his comprehensive knowledge, and clear-eyed view of economic trends, he has been a Cassandra about the looming crises in retirement and healthcare, and deserves to be heard. In the same vein is Peter Peterson's national bestseller, *Running on Empty: How the Democratic and Republican Parties are Bankrupting our Future and What Americans Can Do about It* (New York: Farrar, Straus & Giroux, 2004).

proven to be double-edged swords, benefiting American commerce, but also pushing American jobs overseas and spawning a protectionist backlash. Our nation's technological preeminence is jeopardized, not by the advances of other nations, but by the failings of our educational system and threats to our research and innovation capabilities. A recent poll has found that over 70 percent of the population believes the country is headed in the wrong direction, and approval ratings for the President and the Congress, at the time of this writing, do not break 30 percent.

If we observe the nation confronting these threats, we find a population increasingly divided along partisan lines. The redrawing of Congressional districts has partitioned America into solid red and blue blocs. Wedge issues distract us from more pressing dangers and opportunities. Increasingly, media outlets cater to the self-defined Right and Left, insulating both groups from ideas that would challenge their complacent assumptions. The motto Benjamin Franklin gave us, *E Pluribus Unum*, "out of many, one," doesn't ring quite as true today as it has in our finer hours. If the nation remains as divided as it is today, the new President, regardless of his or her personal courage, intelligence, or charisma, will face the specter of national decline. America needs a "uniter," not just a "decider," before it is too late.

Of course, talk is cheap. Most Presidents have proclaimed the need for unity, civility, and cooperation. In reality, each has struggled to balance the sometimes conflicting roles of Commander-in-Chief, Chief Executive of the nation, and party leader. But between the familiar extremes of high-minded rhetoric and political

> ∾ **Every President has struggled to balance the sometimes conflicting roles of Commander-in-Chief, Chief Executive of the nation, and party leader.**

horse-trading, some Presidents have succeeded in rallying the parties and the nation at crucial points in our history, while others have failed. Too often, Presidents seem ignorant of those who came before them—of the lessons learned, struggles faced, and victories achieved.

In this book, we will make the White House walls talk. We will begin with a survey of instructive tragedies and triumphs of Presidential history. What emerges is a broadly coherent list of the qualities of character and leadership that have allowed Presidents to unite the nation and bring it to new heights. Moving deeper into the links between Presidential past and future, in the second part of this book we will look at the models of Abraham Lincoln and Franklin Roosevelt, our two greatest war leaders. Exploring how they led the nation in times of crisis, we will outline a strategy for leading the nation through a struggle against terrorism during a global age in which America's preeminence is increasingly questioned.

Sustaining Success

In 1987, the English historian Paul Kennedy wrote a widely discussed book, *The Rise and Fall of the Great Powers*.[2] He pointedly took his lead from Edward Gibbon's *History of the Decline and Fall of the Roman Empire*.[3] The book sparked a spirited debate about whether the United States was dissipating its domestic strength by overcommitting its resources abroad. Kennedy's book was hardly the first to argue that overextended powers face certain decline. Thucydides, nearly 2,500 years before, wrote of how Alcibiades led Athenian forces to military disaster in faraway Sicily during the Peloponnesian Wars, and so precipitated the decline of Athens and the rise of its rival Sparta.[4]

Kennedy's book offered a warning, but it was premature. In the buoyant 1980s, we Americans felt on top of the world.

The fall of the Soviet Union and an economic boom in the 1990s contributed to this sense of American triumph. Foreign interventions—a brilliantly successful Persian Gulf War under President George H. W. Bush, and two NATO-fought Balkan interventions during the Clinton presidency—were coupled with financial surpluses at home.

Today, the picture is different. Along with our persistent trade and budget deficits, America spends over $12 billion a month on the wars in Iraq and Afghanistan. Even if troops are withdrawn from Iraq soon, our financial commitment to those countries will remain staggeringly large. Our military forces are overextended and vulnerable. Shiite Iran is on the rise across the region. A viable peace agreement between Israel and the Palestinians remains an unfinished requirement. On our Pacific flank, rising powers could soon herald the Asian century. Reflecting this, Asia is making great strides in education, while our K-12 system continues to fail unacceptably large numbers of students. Global climate change poses a challenge of enormous magnitude, and its costs will be enduring. Paul Kennedy's warning came two decades too early. The next President may arrive in office at the tipping point of American power and influence.

The Lessons of History

Our leaders are fallible, subject to error and hubris, but also capable of great triumphs. Their examples furnish lessons for the next President. Mark Twain observed that "history doesn't repeat itself, but it can rhyme." What will the next President's rhymes be?

This country has survived civil war, two world wars, a protracted nuclear standoff in which the very existence of civilization was threatened, terrorist attacks, and several Presidential assassinations. It has undergone a veritable transformation in its conception of rights and suffrage, moving from a narrowly defined citizenry to the most diverse and assimilated populace on earth. Its history has not always been noble—it is marked by racism, sexism, abuses of power, and periods of mercenary consumerism, which have threatened the shared values that have made this nation a beacon of freedom and opportunity. But in these darker hours, our best leaders have provided a light. They have done so by drawing upon the American experience, and appealing to our best selves in trying to unify the nation to accomplish these challenges.

When Abraham Lincoln took office, the fate of the nation looked grim. Jefferson Davis had been inaugurated as President of the Confederate States of America two weeks earlier. War pitting brother against brother was at hand. But Lincoln, the green "prairie lawyer" and one-term Congressman, did not flinch. In his stirring First Inaugural, he greeted the prospect of a ruptured union with a combination of remorse and resolve, and with the conviction that his mission—and the mission of this nation—had a moral cast. "The mystic chords of memory," he said, "stretching from every battlefield and patriot grave to every living heart and hearthstone all over this broad land, will yet swell the chorus of the Union, when again touched, as surely they will be, by the better angels of our nature."[5]

The mystic chords of memory—it was an appeal to history, as much as to the future. The appeal was more than rhetorical. Lincoln, though regarded as provincial and inexperienced when he took office, understood the powerful lessons offered in the history he had studied, for the country he loved. Above all, he knew from history that if he could not prevent a divided union, he must at least lead a

> ∞ "History doesn't repeat itself, but it can rhyme."
> —*Mark Twain*

united North. Indeed, Lincoln's strategy for winning the Civil War involved first uniting the North while dividing the South. By blockading Southern ports and gaining control of the Mississippi River the Confederacy was split in two. Circumstances are different today than they were 200 years ago, or even 20, but principles of Presidential leadership remain the same. Daunting challenges at home and abroad amount to a crisis as grave as almost any the nation has faced before. But the nation's history offers a rich store of lessons, which any incoming President would be remiss to ignore.

The Center for the Study of the Presidency (CSP) seeks to identify and apply historic lessons to guide the future Presidency in practical ways. Our mission is neither political nor ideological; rather, we seek to preserve and elucidate—for Presidents, their staffs, members of Congress, incumbents, and candidates—the historical memory of Presidential triumphs and tragedies. We believe this counsel must be broader, deeper, and longer range than the advice of policy experts and political consultants who, through no fault of their own, are often distracted by the consuming and corrosive culture of the "permanent campaign."

> ∽ **Daunting challenges at home and abroad amount to a crisis as grave as almost any the nation has faced before. But the nation's history offers a rich store of lessons, which any incoming President would be remiss to ignore.**

In 1999, when it was reestablished and reorganized in Washington, CSP published a series of seventy-six case studies in Presidential history. This earlier book examined the successes and failures of the modern Presidency and was made available to both Presidential candidates prior to the 2000 election and the transition.[6]

The Center examined all interventions and reconstructions since President Dwight Eisenhower's decision not to intervene in the 1954 Indo-China crisis.[7]* The Center's report on *Comprehensive Strategic Reform* called for reorganizing and strengthening the entire national security process in order to better anticipate and prepare for contingencies. Another report examined how science and technology should be reorganized to foster greater innovation and national competitiveness.[8] Around the same time, the United States Commission on National Security released the Hart-Rudman Report, a broad look at strategies for addressing likely political, social, economic, and environmental changes over the next twenty-five years.

This book draws on these and other publications, including *Presidential Studies Quarterly*, the nation's premier journal on the American Presidency, which is edited by forty leading Presidential historians. I will also draw occasionally on my own experiences, particularly in the field of Executive-Legislative relations and from my time leading the CSP and the Center for Strategic and International Studies.

In the coming months, the Center will also supplement the findings and recommendations in this book with focus group discussions, involving leading thinkers and policymakers from in and outside of Washington, on subject areas such as repairing damaged geopolitical relations, rebuilding the military, K-12 education, the Social Security and Medicare crises, runaway healthcare costs, and the need to accelerate investments in science and medicine.

---

*When CSP provided incoming President George W. Bush's staff with this report, we were told that the new Administration would not be intervening or involved in the kind of "nation-building" seen under the Clinton Administration. September 11 changed these priorities dramatically.

A final note. As someone who came to Washington for graduate work in 1957 but was subsequently in the public policy field in and out of government, writing this book has often been a sensitive task. Many sections deal with still-living individuals and at times cut across past and current friendships. But if this book were not loyal, first and foremost, to the next President and the future success of that office, the effort would lose its integrity. The judgments in this document, of course, are my responsibility alone and not those of the Center as an institution.

For the next President, I would certainly offer the advice Benjamin Franklin gave when he urged his fellow delegates at Philadelphia to ratify the Constitution: "I cannot help expressing a wish that every member of the convention who may still have objections to [the Constitution] would, with me on this occasion doubt a little of his own infallibility...."⁹ I have certainly doubted my own, on more than one occasion, in preparing this perhaps overly ambitious document.

A House without Memory

For every Administration, on Inauguration Day, the clock of history is reset. The White House has no archives in residence, and the desk drawers are cleaned out for the new Administration. New Presidents are often eager to throw off history and start afresh, rebuilding government and the nation according to promises made on the campaign trail. The White House has always lacked a meaningful institutional memory. I learned this firsthand. In early January 1987, as then-NATO Ambassador, I was suddenly summoned to the White House by President Ronald Reagan to serve for three months as his Special Counselor on the Iran-Contra affair.

> The White House lacks a meaningful institutional memory.

My duties were to report directly to the President, help coordinate the investigations, and restore integrity to the White House. At the same time, President Reagan had also set up an investigative board, led by Senators John Tower and Edmund Muskie and General Brent Scowcroft, to conduct a two-month review of what had gone wrong with the National Security Council process, and to recommend to the President corrective action. I had something to contribute to their reexamination: a highly relevant past. In the mid-1970s, I spent two years on a blue ribbon Presidential commission chaired by Ambassador Robert Murphy and including Governor Nelson Rockefeller and Senate Majority Leader Mike Mansfield. The commission focused on, among other things, improving the process of decision-making in the National Security Council, as well as Executive-Legislative branch relations. When the report was delivered to President Gerald R. Ford, I received a letter from him saying how valuable this study would be to future Presidents. In January of 1987, my copy of the report was in storage, so I asked the White House staff for this esteemed Murphy Commission Report. The following day, the word came back: "Don't have it. In fact, never heard of it."

I also wanted to research another relevant Presidential crisis—President John F. Kennedy's role in the Bay of Pigs debacle and how Kennedy rebounded from his dramatic setback. Again, the White House replied they had "no record." Presidents and their staffs *should* have a record of the past. At the very least, it should be accessible, thorough, yet not overly detailed, and not far from their desks. We hope that this book, to some extent, fulfills all of these criteria.

CHAPTER 2

ELEMENTS OF PRESIDENTIAL LEADERSHIP

WHAT WERE the leadership requirements for our next President? A beginning can be found in the *Federalist Paper #70*, which speaks of a vigorous executive, active but thoroughly republican.* Our first President was the embodiment of this. George Washington had sheer

---

* Anne Marie Slaughter defines the difference in the historic use of the terms republican and democratic, by contrasting two statements: Alexander Hamilton's 1787 assertion at the Constitution Convention "We are a republican government. Real liberty is never found in despotism or in the extremes of democracy," with George W. Bush's "Democracy is on the march" speech (September 3, 2004). As Slaughter notes, "For its first century, America did not promise democracy to its people, and was not in the Declaration or the Constitution. Washington, Madison, and Hamilton perceived great differences between a democracy and a republic. A republic "was a government on which votes must elect people to represent them. Democracy, however, meant pure majority rule. Democracy today means self-government by all citizens, which means, above all, granting all citizens the right to vote." (Anne Marie Slaughter, *The Idea That Is America: Keeping Faith with Our Values in a Dangerous World*, [New York: Basic Books, 2007], pp. 45–47). As we shall later note, this right to vote for all Americans did not occur until the Voting Rights Act of 1965.

physical size and presence. He was a military hero and an excellent manager. But what made him stand apart was his absolute integrity and his conviction that the good of the country was paramount. He believed deeply in civility, which to him meant, in part, a spirit of inclusiveness.* As historian Gordon Wood wrote in his book *Revolutionary Characters*, "Washington's genius, Washington's greatness, lay in his character." It did not come automatically.[1] He worked hard to cultivate Enlightenment values—copying out 110 maxims from the *Rules of Civility and Decent Behaviour in Company and Conversation*, for example, and watching Joseph Addison's play *Cato* repeatedly.[2] Comparisons between the theater and the new America were not lost on him. He fostered a healthy appreciation of being watched, as though on the world stage, as he and his countrymen enacted an experiment in liberty. He transformed himself to fill the role, and in doing so, transformed the nation to consist of an effective and potentially powerful office of the Presidency.

George Washington, along with cabinet members Thomas Jefferson (Secretary of State) and Alexander Hamilton (Secretary of the Treasury), practiced what leadership experts call "transformational leadership." Rather than improving society at the margins—"transactional leadership"—he produced revolutionary change in the very way that Americans understood themselves and their nation.** This is literally true—Washington was

---

*In 2006, after the civility and integrity failures of the last Congress, CSP developed the *Mount Vernon Compact* for members of Congress to sign to revive Washington's standards.

**My concept of transformational leadership draws from James MacGregor Burns's seminal *Leadership* (New York: Harper & Row, 1978). Definitions of transformational and transactional leadership are much debated, but I have used the terms to appeal to a general difference between "management," which responds to day-to-day

the great leader of the Revolutionary War—but true in a deeper sense as well. Following the break with Britain, his leadership gave stability, credibility, and guidance to an experiment in liberty, which could easily have collapsed from infighting or European interference.

George Washington was not America's only transformational leader. Later, Andrew Jackson transformed the party process and empowered the common man. Abraham Lincoln completed the second American Revolution, reimaging the mandate of the country—the idea that men are "created equal." Theodore Roosevelt's progressive movement, Franklin Roosevelt's New Deal, Lyndon Johnson's Great Society, and Ronald Reagan's vision of a world without the Soviet Union were all transformational objectives.

> At certain turning points, Presidents have the opportunity to change the national landscape with bold new strokes. Our current moment in history is one such turning point.

At certain turning points, Presidents have the opportunity to change the national landscape with bold new strokes. Our current moment in history is one such turning point. As the next President prepares for transformational leadership, he or she would benefit from a brief survey of the office of the Presidency. This series of portraits is not meant to be comprehensive. Rather it is meant to highlight the successes and failures of key Presidents—some well known, some less

---

challenges to maintain and marginally improve capabilities and resources while defusing conflicts, and what I would call "transformational leadership," which enacts visionary social or political change. For the management/leadership distinction, see Abraham Zaleznik, "Managers and Leaders: Are They Different?" *Harvard Business Review* (55.5, 1977), pp. 67–78.

so—that are most relevant to the challenges that will face our next Commander-in-Chief. The narrative that follows will culminate in a discussion of seven qualities of character and leadership needed in the man or woman America elects in 2008. Our new President must be able to unite a nation in crisis and mobilize it in the name of a common cause, both domestically and internationally. This will require the trust of Congress and the nation, as well as respected party leadership. Indispensable to our next leader will be a courageous nature tempered by a healthy wariness against hubris, an organized Executive branch and talented, focused cabinet of advisors, and a transformational vision backed up by a comprehensive, long-term grand strategy. After a brief discussion of these qualities at the end of the narrative, we will address, in Part II, the six elements of grand strategy that the next President will need to address our range of challenges at home and abroad.

CHAPTER 3

PRESIDENTIAL PORTRAITS

George Washington: The Model President

Washington was neither a great intellectual nor a great legislator. Although an inspiring battlefield commander, he lacked the strategic genius of Napoleon Bonaparte or Arthur Wellesley, the Duke of Wellington. Yet he was among our greatest Chief Executives, and, though it is less well known, was also a brilliant manager of the new federal government. According to Douglas Southall Freeman, Washington learned to lead large organizations in his early years as master of the Mount Vernon plantation. Among the Colonial Virginia estates, Mount Vernon was a successful, money-making enterprise (albeit with the use of slaves, a fact which plagued Washington throughout his life; although he set them free at his death, the memory will forever dog his legacy).[1] George Washington's self-control and self-confidence gave him an unsurpassed ability to attract and marshal talent. Comfortable in his skin, he rarely felt diminished as he surrounded himself with people whom he considered more brilliant than himself.

Tobias Lear, his private secretary, served a role similar to the modern-day White House Chief of Staff. He helped to make sure that Washington was exposed to a diversity of voices and not isolated in a bubble of sycophantic staff and advisors. (At one time or another in their Presidencies, Woodrow

Wilson, Lyndon Johnson, Richard Nixon, Ronald Reagan, and George W. Bush were all caught in such a bubble.) But far more important than Lear was Washington himself, who wisely included in his Cabinet two political opposites: Secretary of State Thomas Jefferson, champion of the agrarian republic of virtue, and Secretary of the Treasury Alexander Hamilton, champion of fiscal responsibility, commerce, and cosmopolitanism.

Both geniuses, Jefferson and Hamilton stood on separate sides of the most divisive issue of the day: whether the national government should assume the debts incurred by the states during the Revolution. Jefferson rejected debt assumption; Hamilton favored it, along with import tariffs and excise taxes to foot the bill. As historian Ronald Chernow writes, in 1790 the quarrels "grew so vitriolic that it didn't seem far-fetched that the union might break up over the issue."[2] Basic assumptions about the nature and extent of central government— which many had believed the colonies had fought to free themselves from—were at stake. However, with Hamilton's Federalists and Jefferson's Democratic Republicans equally matched, and deadlock looming, civility prevailed.

Jefferson invited Hamilton to what proved to be one of the nation's most fruitful dinner parties, and before the courses were completed, Jefferson agreed that the government would assume the Revolutionary War debts of the states by the federal government in exchange for moving the National Capital to its present location on the Potomac. Biased toward Hamilton's view, President Washington was pleased, for he, like modern Presidents Dwight Eisenhower and Bill Clinton, knew that the solvency of this nation was a critical factor in its survival. Within a few years, the economy was booming, aided by European capital, Hamilton's financial genius, and Jefferson's grand bargain.

As often as Washington is lionized as our Founding Father, we often forget that this involved not only a great feat of public leadership but also a feat of institutional management. After choosing a cabinet designed to hold together a fragile union, Washington oversaw the creation of the U.S. government's first institutions not provided for in the Constitution: the Departments of State, War, Treasury, and Justice. Organizing and staffing these offices was a massive project, which might easily have gone awry without Washington's sturdy and even-handed leadership.[*]

He also set an example of how to deal with one of the sensitive subjects in American politics: the place of religion in public life. Though he believed that "Religion and Morality are indispensable supports" of "political prosperity,"[3] he upheld the separation of church and state and fervently championed religious freedom. His intention was not to exclude religion from politics, but rather to enrich religion by protecting individual denominations and faiths from overpowering one another—and to prevent the state from overpowering religion in general, as it had in England. Washington was a communicant and vestryman of the Episcopal Church, but he set the example by attending services with Catholics, Baptists, and Presbyterians and communicating with Quakers as well as the historic Touro Synagogue in Newport, Rhode Island. After meeting with members of this Hebrew congregation he wrote to them, saying, "May the children of the stock of Abraham, who dwell in this land, continue to merit and enjoy the good will of the other inhabitants while everyone shall sit in safety under his own vine and fig tree and there shall be none to

---

[*] While George Washington himself had perhaps the most informal schooling of any President, aside from Lincoln, he developed an intense interest in education and bequeathed the land for the present Washington & Lee University in Lexington, Virginia, as well as Washington College in Chestertown, Maryland and the Primary School for Orphan Education in Alexandria, Virginia.

make him afraid."[4] Religious freedom rang clear. Although Washington clearly expressed his personal faith when in combat, he believed as Lincoln did, that he had no direct line to the Almighty for guidance on matters of public policy. He may well have agreed with Lincoln's view that Americans were God's "almost chosen people"—blessed with freedom, but no less prone than other nations to its abuse.

Washington's tolerant religious views reinforced his fear of factionalism and his opposition to the formation of political parties. The partisan excesses of today would horrify him. Indeed, he was appalled even in his own day, when two parties sprung up and the rhetorical mudslinging began. John Adams and Thomas Jefferson engaged in smear campaigns that would have impressed today's tabloids.

John Adams, Washington's successor, would see one of the most divisive periods in our history. Incivility and polarization were inflamed by a conflict with the revolutionary government of France, whose war ships and privateers harassed our maritime trade. It was during Adams's Administration that the nation would experience its first disagreements over "Presidential war powers," an area of Executive authority that would have a long and often undistinguished history, even into our own day. Adams considered declaring war against France, but opted for a special session with Congress that rescinded all treaties with France and authorized attacks on French vessels. Thus began the nation's first foreign military engagement since independence, a so-called quasi-war with France.

> "Every difference of opinion is not a difference of principle,"
> —*Thomas Jefferson*

The Constitution was a new and fragile thing. During Adams's Administration it came under assault with the passage of the Alien and Sedition Acts, in blatant contradiction to the First Amendment right of free speech, and the XYZ Affair, in which French agents attempted to extort money from U.S. diplomats as the price of negotiating a treaty with France. Already, it was clear that there were differing opinions of how to interpret and apply constitutional powers, especially in the face of threats to the nation's security—even among the Founding Fathers, the very people who had brought that document into being. But Adams played a crucial role in protecting the infant nation from a full-scale war with France. He paid a political price for it, however, and only served one term.

Thomas Jefferson: Chief Executive, Party Leader, and Innovator

The new President, Thomas Jefferson, strove to be a "unifier." He needed to be. The 1800 election had been deadlocked in the Electoral College, forcing the House of Representatives to intervene. Jefferson recognized his mandate was fragile and reached out to the opposition. In his inaugural address, Jefferson spoke of unity. "Every difference of opinion is not a difference of principle," he said. "We have called by different names brethren of the same principle. We are all Republicans. We are all Federalists." The importance of this message—coming from a President who was accused of taking party leadership more seriously than national leadership—cannot be overstated.

It is also worth touching on Jefferson's encouragement of science and innovation as crucial to the nation's power. As a scientist and inventor himself, he entered office with a conviction that science occupied a crucial role in our national strength and our diplomatic relations. As President, he made an extraordinary investment into scientific inquiry. He sent Lewis and Clark on their famous expedition and drew attention to their discoveries, displaying what they brought back on the National Mall and at Monticello. After leaving office, he designed and established the University of Virginia. Our next President should assume Jefferson's mantle as a robust supporter of education, technology, and science, especially in light of the great strides competitors like China and India have made in these fields (as well as the urgent need for renewable sources of energy).

In other ways, Jefferson sought restraint. He entered office with modest ambitions for the government he was about to lead. He favored smaller government, military and naval disarmament, states rights, decentralization, and agrarian society virtues. He expressed contempt for the militant nationalists who sought to concentrate power in the hands of the executive. Yet he was not dogmatic, and when new circumstances forced him to get hawkish, he did. He refused "tribute money" to the pirates of Tripoli, and without Congressional consent sent a naval squadron to the Mediterranean. He founded the United States Military Academy. He authorized the second-largest territorial expansion in American history, the Louisiana Purchase. He may not have intended to radically expand the reach of the government, but he did. The unexpected opportunities of his day required bold new thinking, and he seized the moment.[*]

Riding a wave of popularity after the Louisiana Purchase, Jefferson won reelection in 1804. But his second term was not as successful as his first, an experience well known by modern two-term Presidents such as Woodrow Wilson, Dwight Eisen-

---

[*] After leaving office, Jefferson and his erstwhile enemy, John Adams, reconciled and struck up a magnificent correspondence, filled with some of the most profound reflections on political theory, history, and the early Republic. Interestingly, they both died on the same day, July 4, 1826. That tradition of Presidential civility has been rejuvenated in our time by the collaborative efforts of ex-Presidents Jimmy Carter and Gerald Ford, and Bill Clinton and George H. W. Bush.

hower, Bill Clinton, and George W. Bush. Angered by French and British abuses of American ships on the high seas, Jefferson enacted an embargo on all trade in and out of the United States. He wanted to teach Europe to respect American rights but ended up harming the U.S. economy and incurring the wrath of our commercial interests. In this, he was his own worst enemy—which makes him, again, similar to many recent Presidents.

James Madison: Great Legislator and Failed War Leader

Rivalries with Britain and France over trade and territory continued into James Madison's administration, culminating with the War of 1812, the most disastrous and poorly planned engagement of our history. Hawks such as John C. Calhoun and Speaker of the House Henry Clay sought war as a means of acquiring land in Canada and Western Florida, and they vowed to turn against Madison, a fellow Republican, if he backed down from the fight.* Madison, for his part, was conflicted about his powers to initiate and execute war,

---

* Initial debates on the wording of the Constitution gave Congress the power to "make" war rather than to just "declare" it. However, Elbridge Gerry questioned what would happen if the United States was attacked while the Congress was out of session. Therefore, after a unanimous vote, the language was changed to reflect Congress's ability to "declare" war, leaving the power to "make" or conduct war to the Executive (Jacob K. Javits, *Who Makes War: The President versus Congress* [New York: William Morrow & Company, Inc., 1973], pp. 13–15). President Madison was a delegate at the Convention and had a front row seat during this debate. The Madison Administration was the first in the history of the United States to declare war on another country. The contention that Madison was pushed into the war by the war-hawks is challenged by Garry Wills (*James Madison* [New York: Times Books, 2002] p. 96).

while Federalists were fiercely opposed to an engagement of any kind. Some New England states even refused to commit their militias. Detroit fell early to the British and a grand three-pronged ground offensive into Canada succeeded mostly in enraging the Canadians, when a U.S. force sacked and burned Toronto. America's only decisive land victory, Andrew Jackson's battle of New Orleans, took place after a peace treaty had been signed (though it did have the effect of energizing the nation, giving a frustrating slog a victorious coda). By the end of the war, our nation's capital had been burned and the government was deep in debt.

Madison learned from his war failure. He responded swiftly to accusations that the "Scholar President" was weak on national security and financially incompetent. In a brilliant turnaround (perhaps a lesson for Democrats today) he and his successor James Monroe moved to restart the National Bank, build up the Navy and coastal defense, and lay the groundwork for a scheme of turnpikes and canals stretching across the eastern regions. This necessary but dramatic shift within the party platform appalled the aging Jefferson.

James Monroe added to Madison's legacy of muscular nationalism. In 1823, he announced that the free and independent American continents would resist colonization by European powers. This guiding principle, known as the Monroe Doctrine, represented a bold declaration for a fledgling nation.[5] It also highlighted America's complicated and sometimes contradictory vision of itself and its place in the world: a nation wary of interference, but seizing a large sphere of influence; a nation willing to stand up to world powers, but desiring peace. At home, Monroe presided over the "Era of Good Feelings," holding civility high in the public sphere. American recovery from the War of 1812 offers an example of American resilience that may be instructive as America looks to heal the wounds from the Iraq War.

Even as the country was solidifying its position with respect to Europe, cracks were forming and spreading at home. No candidate won a majority of electoral votes in the Election of 1824, and the contest was thrown into the House of Representatives. There, Henry Clay of Kentucky (Speaker of the House and also [...] who had finished fourth in the election) instructed [...] to switch their votes to John Quincy Adams, who [...] Secretary of State. Followers of the loser, [...], termed the election a "corrupt bargain." Clay [...] come the "Great Compromiser," brokering the [...] 820 and 1850, and therefore keeping a tenu- [...] North and South—but he never achieved [...] which he so desperately craved.

Andrew Jackson: Union Above All

Andrew Jackson, however, got his chance, four years later. The Tennessee war hero was a controversial figure in his time, and in our own. Fiery and at times petulant, with a tendency to equate personal loyalty with patriotism, his legacy was mixed— the relocation of Native Americans on the "Trail of Tears" being the most obvious tragedy of his administration. Nevertheless, Jackson enlarged the reach of democracy by supporting the extension of the vote to all white males, regardless of whether they owned property. Called "King Mob," he was the first populist President and dispensed patronage generously to the backwoodsmen who invaded the White House "hooting and hollering" on Inauguration Day. The late Arthur Schlesinger Jr., whose brilliant *Age of Jackson* marked the beginning of a long and distinguished career as a public historian, saw Jackson as a wellspring to the age of Roosevelt and the New Deal.[6] He was the first to emphasize the people's interests before those of the powerful. "The people are sovereign," he declared. "They can alter or amend."

Jackson was able to stand his ground, even against his own political base when the need arose. When South Carolina, led by Vice President John C. Calhoun, attempted to nullify a federal tariff, citing states' rights, an angry Jackson alerted military forces and averred that "Hamon's gallows were not high enough to hang" his erstwhile colleague. Though a supporter of states' rights, Jackson saw that South Carolina's move threatened to splinter the country. Where Clay was a compromiser, Jackson was decisive. The times required both. Today, Jackson's statue, which dominates the square in front of the White House, is engraved with his statement: "The union, it must be preserved." These are inspiring words for the next President, who like Jackson will lead a country torn by sectional and ideological differences.

James Polk: Masterful War Leader, Charged with Deception

The Mexican War (1846-1848) affords a case study on a timely topic: Presidential war powers. In initiating and executing the war, James Polk claimed authorities exceeding even those claimed by the Bush-Cheney White House. In the years preceding the conflict, border disputes between Mexico and the recently annexed state of Texas had been endemic. Polk dealt with the problem by moving troops into the disputed territory and then announcing that the Mexicans had fired on U.S. soldiers within U.S. territory. Polk never asked Congress to declare war; rather, with troops already mobilized, he simply asked them to recognize that a state of war already existed.

Abraham Lincoln, a freshman Whig Representative from Illinois at the time, was irate, and attributed the affair to Polk's hunger for "military glory, that attractive rainbow, that rises in showers of blood." Speaking on the House floor, Lincoln demanded that the President identify the exact "spot" where the attack on American soil had occurred (this would later earn him the moniker "spotty Lincoln"). He called the war "unnecessary and unconstitutional" and charged the President with "deception." In these criticisms—along with those of Daniel Webster and John C. Calhoun, who also opposed the war—one can hear echoes of arguments raised over George W. Bush's invasion of Iraq in 2003.

Unlike the present Iraq War, however, the Mexican War was a relatively swift and decisive victory, owing in part to Polk's keen sense of wartime strategy. Polk, indeed, stands as one of the more skilled, if not constitutionally sensitive, Presidents in our history. The Mexican Concessions increased national territory by one third, including the harbors of San Diego and San Francisco, and stoked the fervor for America's "manifest destiny." As journalist John O'Sullivan intoned: "Yes, more and more . . . till our national destiny is fulfilled and the whole boundless continent is ours."[7] The question of whether and how to expand slavery into these new territories would help prepare the road to the Civil War.

The slavery issue reached boiling point during the administration of James Buchanan. Buchanan, a former minister to Russia and Great Britain and Secretary of State, came to office as one of the most well-credentialed Presidents of the nineteenth century. But his example illustrates that experience is not necessarily a harbinger of future success. Buchanan was woefully ineffective. Neither a compromiser nor a decisionmaker, he was paralyzed by the growing threat of secession. The opposite, in some ways, of James Polk, he was convinced that the President lacked the Constitutional authority to stop the union from dissolving. As he left office, he is said to have told the incoming President, Abraham Lincoln: "If you are as happy, my dear sir, in entering this house as I am in leaving it and returning home, you are the happiest man in the country."[8]

Abraham Lincoln: Our Genius

Lincoln lacked Buchanan's impressive resume. Before 1860, he was a frontier lawyer who had served two weeks as militia Captain in the Black Hawk War and one term in Congress. But he arguably proved to be the greatest transformational President in American history. He put us on the pathway to completing the "second American revolution."* He had a rare genius—the ability to adhere to a grand vision, yet act pragmatically. He knew that the best route to his goal was not always the shortest.

> ∾ Lincoln is arguably the greatest President in the nation's history and his example is the best one for future Presidents.

The literature on Lincoln extends for miles, touching on almost every aspect of his multifaceted character, from his rhetorical abilities and war strategy, to his compassion and resolve. Recently, in her book *Team of Rivals*, Doris Kearns Goodwin explored Lincoln's often contentious Cabinet, which he designed to hold together a politically divided North. As Goodwin describes, "Lincoln's political genius revealed through his extraordinary array of personal qualities . . . enabled him to form friendships with men who [had] previously opposed him; to repair injured feelings, that, left unmentioned, might have escalated into permanent hostility; to assume responsibility for failure of subordinates; to share credit with ease; and to learn from mistakes. . . ."[9] This is remarkable, useful advice for the next President of the United States.

---

* This phrase is the subject of James M. McPherson's book, *Abraham Lincoln and the Second American Revolution* (New York: Oxford University Press, 1991). As McPherson notes, the new birth of freedom declared at Gettysburg was not completed until the era of Martin Luther King Jr. and Lyndon Baines Johnson.

But it was empathy on a greater, more profound scale that brought Lincoln to the heights of his Second Inaugural Address. He did not flaunt his unconventional faith, but he was undoubtedly the greatest religious mind ever to occupy the White House. He had a reconciling and public-minded form of Biblical belief that allowed him to ask his countrymen, during Civil War, to show "malice toward none" and "charity for all." And yet he balanced this call for civility with a call for "firmness in the right as God gives us to see the right," as pithy an expression of dedication and courage as there has ever been in Presidential history.[10]

At the same time, Lincoln could be tough. He assumed extensive war powers while Congress was out of session, by increasing the regular army (a Congressional prerogative) and suspending *habeas corpus*. He would later take over telegraph and railroad lines and issue the Emancipation Proclamation, which was termed an "expropriation without compensation of private property."[11] Summing up his view on war powers, Lincoln declared: "I think the Constitution invests its Commander-in-Chief with the laws of war in time of war."[12] It is crucial to note that a "time of war" like the one Lincoln's generation witnessed has not, with the exception of World War II, been experienced since. His ruthless measures would no doubt have backfired had the nation not been involved in a total war on its own soil.

Even with the country at war with itself, Lincoln was able to keep the broad view of national power in perspective, thinking beyond the military conflict to national greatness. Like Thomas Jefferson, he gave crucial support to science and technology.

> Even in the midst of Civil War, Lincoln was able to keep the broad view of national power in perspective, thinking beyond the military conflict to national greatness.

Lincoln backed land-grant colleges through the Morrill Act and established the National Academies of Sciences. As a former railroad lawyer in Illinois, he understood how vital this new form of transportation was to the economic future of the nation, and he signed a bill chartering the first transcontinental railroad.

Like George Washington, Lincoln could see the nation as a unique experiment, fragile at times, carried out not just for the sake of Americans, but for all mankind. The world watched to see if this novel project, "dedicated to the proposition that all men are created equal," would succeed or fail. This sense of being steward of a larger enterprise, as much as being leader of a people, helped Lincoln to craft some of his greatest achievements of oratory, such as the Gettysburg Address. Fittingly, he became an enormous figure in Europe and eventually around the world; Leo Tolstoy believed "his example is universal and will last thousands of years."[13] In part, Lincoln had his era to thank: the upheaval of Civil War pushed American vulnerability to the fore, tearing away the illusions of grandeur which often lead to Presidential hubris.

The next President would do well to study Lincoln's insights from a troubled time. Great moments in our history have emerged not only from confidence in our values, but also from the recognition of how elusive these can be.

Andrew Johnson, Ulysses Grant, Rutherford Hayes, and William McKinley: Presidencies in Turmoil

Abraham Lincoln was not an easy act to follow, but his successors were failures by any standards. The callous Tennessean Andrew Johnson actually underwent impeachment proceedings by an equally uncompromising Congress. General Ulysses S. Grant, the hero of the Grand Army of the Republic, entered office with hyperbolic hopes. An honest man himself, his

Administration was plagued by scandal and corruption. This should be a lesson for future Presidents: those who surround you have the potential to ruin you.

Scandals did not end with Grant's term. The 1876 election, which pitted Rutherford B. Hayes against Samuel Tilden, was so strongly disputed that the country verged on another civil war. Hayes lost the popular vote, but won the Presidency through the Compromise of 1877, in which he agreed to end military occupation in the South and choose former Confederate Colonel David McKendree Key as his Postmaster General. As Senator, Key pushed for North-South reconciliation and staunchly opposed the idea of a "solid South" based on white hegemony. In his Inaugural address, Hayes declared that "he serves his party best who serves his country," and later toured the South with Key to promote reconciliation.[*]

In 1896, William McKinley brought Presidential elections into the modern age. His shrewd campaign manager, Mark

---

[*] Parts of the Compromise of 1877 were controversial, but that did not inhibit its passage. First, the South was designated to receive a portion of railway subsidies then going solely to the North. Second, because democracy in the South could not be based on occupation indefinitely, Union troops would be withdrawn from the South, which could be interpreted as abandoning the former slaves still there. However, continued occupation would not have prevented the white racist populists of the 1880s (nor the former planter class of the Reconstruction) who passed the Jim Crow laws and built the color line across the South. (David Key, subsequently a federal circuit judge, railed against this later development.) The downside of this attempted reconciliation was that civil rights laws passed in 1868 and the Fifteenth Amendment were not enforced in the South, and two hundred thousand African-Americans who fought with Grant were deprived of their rights, as historians Eric Foner and James McPherson have vividly written. This story was part of the author's published dissertation, titled *The South Rejects a Prophet: The Life of Senator D. M. Kelly, 1824–1900* (Washington, DC: Praeger Publishers, 1967).

Hanna, produced the coalition that brought Republicans back to the White House and gave them majorities in Congress. As Hanna raised mountains of campaign money, McKinley attacked his opponent, William Jennings Bryan, as a threat to the economy. Theodore Roosevelt remarked that Hanna "has advertised McKinley as if he were a patent medicine." One could see the McKinley-Hanna partnership as a predecessor to the Bush-Rove relationship of our day—and of all political consultants who play such a large role in contemporary politics.[14]*

McKinley initially opposed going to war with Spain over Cuba. But after the sinking of the U.S. battleship *Maine* in Havana harbor (almost certainly an accident) was cast by imperial-minded "yellow journalists" as a Spanish plot, popular sentiment left him little choice.[15]** The war brought fame to the man who would later serve as McKinley's Vice President, Theodore Roosevelt. He, like McKinley, had a keen sense of public relations, and turned himself into an American hero by charging with the "Rough Riders" up San Juan Hill in a new Brooks Brothers uniform.

Theodore Roosevelt: Warrior, Progressive

As President, Roosevelt was a complicated figure. He was a patrician, Harvard-educated author of dozens of books, but he was also a progressive, unlike McKinley and Hanna. His compassion was generous and real. As police commissioner, he read the muckraking journalism of Jacob Riis and wrote him a note,

---

* Rove supports the thesis that McKinley, not Hanna, was the architect of this political revolution.

** In 1976, an inquiry led by Admiral Hyman Rickover concluded that in fact the USS *Maine* was sunk from an internal explosion—a consequence of an ill-ventilated coal bunker igniting an adjoining magazine.

saying, "I am here to help." And he was—cleaning up the tenements and the streets of New York City. He fought corruption, "busting trusts" with the same vigor he hunted bears out West. He started the environmentalist movement and laid out a program for regulating and preserving America's natural resources. He restored trust in government, at a time when public confidence had ebbed amidst scandal. He spurred the building of the Panama Canal, an engineering feat. He received the Nobel Prize after presiding over the 1905 Peace Agreement, concluding the Russo-Japanese War, was a mediator between Germany and France in their dispute over Morocco, and sent our "Great White Fleet" sailing around the world to demonstrate American naval prowess.

Often bullheaded and difficult, Roosevelt could be a loose cannon. But he also knew how to gain the respect of even those who opposed him. It was McKinley's death, not an election, which first brought him to power, but he worked with Congress to gain a sense of legitimacy in the eyes of the nation. His vision combined the (traditionally Republican) importance of strength abroad—he doubled the size of the Navy, for example—with (traditionally Democratic) progressive reform. Plainly, Roosevelt expanded the power of the Presidency, particularly in seizing Panama. But he did so openly and with the trust of the American people, whereas Presidents before and after him have usually increased executive power on the sly, producing Congressional backfire. The way Roosevelt put it, "the constitution did not explicitly give me the power to do what I did—it did not forbid me to do what I did.... Therefore, I did my best to get the Senate to ratify what I had done.... I took Panama"[16] and it was up to them to sign off on it.

One beneficiary of this period of national expansion, from the Panama Canal to the Spanish and American War, was the field of health. Just before the war, the Army surgeon and bacteriologist, Walter Reed, carried out breakthrough research in the bacteriology of erysipelas and diphtheria. In 1898, he and others moved forward against typhoid fever and eliminated yellow fever in the United States and Cuba. This was the beginning of breakthroughs which, though initiated by the military, brought about great leaps in public health. In subsequent years, U.S. funding would help in the development of antibiotics and other sulfa drugs. We will return to the strategic importance of supporting medical research in Part II, and how military innovation can have multiple effects in civil society in general.

Woodrow Wilson: Rigid Scholar and Visionary

Woodrow Wilson, like Roosevelt, didn't come to office with a strong mandate. He was elected with a minority vote, but he gained control of both Houses and used it to good effect. He passed progressive measures that built new institutions for governance, such as the Owens-Glass Act of 1913, the first recognition of the national banking system since the Civil War, and the Federal Trade Commission Act in 1914, to prevent unfair methods of competition in interstate commerce. He also strengthened the Clayton Antitrust Act. With war raging in Europe in 1916, he laid before Congress a new preparedness plan including a reserve officer training corps, and he toured the country to promote it. With the April 6, 1917, declaration of war triggered by German submarine attacks, the American expedition under General John J. Pershing saved exhausted France.

Wilson offered an inspiring vision for world peace and democratic governance with his ringing "Fourteen Points." They read like poetry. This former President of Princeton University and eminent scholar proved to be the great idealist, appealing to an almost utopian vision of the world. This idealism—harkening back to the idea of America as a beacon for the world—remains a dominant strain in the nation's self-perception, taken up with enthusiasm by recent neoconservatives. But however stirring Wilson's moral appeal, it could not save him from his rigid refusal to work in a bipartisan way with Congress or his rival Senator Henry Cabot Lodge.

The author of a 2000 Center for the Study of the Presidency case study, John Milton Cooper, writes that Wilson's failure to gain Senate consent to the Treaty of Versailles "... stands to this day as the greatest Presidential failure in the politics of foreign policy" and that this supreme error offers a number of lessons for any future President. First, Wilson did not practice bipartisanship. He could have appointed a Republican to the negotiating delegation that went to Versailles, but he didn't. "Like most strong Presidents, Wilson commanded these errors out of the defect of his own virtues. He was a singularly bold leader and wanted to preserve as much freedom as possible." Second, he was unwilling to compromise in negotiations with the Senate. This led Lodge, who was initially open to some aspects of the Treaty, to become leader of an intransigent bipartisan opposition. Paradoxically, a majority of the nation wanted to see the Treaty ratified. But it was not to be: Wilson suffered a stroke in 1919 and his wife Edith and aide Joe Tumulty truly put him in a bubble and prevented any last chance for negotiation with the Senate. The ailing Wilson later complained that the Senate's failure to ratify the League of Nations "broke the heart of the world."[17]

Franklin D. Roosevelt: The New Deal and Mobilizing for War

In 1933, Franklin Roosevelt inherited a country lost in the Great Depression. His predecessor, Herbert Hoover, was talented but ultimately unable to extricate the country from the paralyzing economic crisis. Roosevelt knew something about overcoming odds. In 1923, he was struck with polio, paralyzing him from the waist down. Before his illness, he had been considered something of a playboy—handsome, rich, a light-weight at Harvard. "F.D." was said to stand for "feather duster." His illness, coupled with a growing social awareness, changed him. It made him both tougher and more compassionate. A decade later, in 1933, he gave his most moving speech. "The only thing we have to fear is fear itself," he told a crippled nation, inspiring the hope and trust of the public. He knew from his own experience that people can draw on hidden reserves of strength.

Pledging a New Deal for the common man, a confident, optimistic leader was about to inspire a desperate nation. In his "first one hundred days" in office, Roosevelt met the crisis with rapid-fire legislation. As historian James MacGregor Burns writes, he started reforming "with no set program or even definite philosophy of government."[18] His first step was to stem a run on the banks by closing all banks for four days and calling Congress into session for banking reform legislation. The next three months saw further emergency relief, including the ingenious Civilian Conservation Corps (CCC), which, by 1940 would put two million unemployed Americans to work on infrastructure renewal projects like road- and bridge-building, reforestation, flood control, and building construction.

This sound measure was followed by a few missteps, including the overly restrictive codes and controls incorporated into the National Industrial Recovery Act (NRA). When the Supreme Court ruled that the federal government had overstepped its authority,[19] Roosevelt responded with legislation that would allow him to "pack the court" with judges sympathetic to

⮞ **Roosevelt was strong because he knew his weaknesses. He was a poor manager, so he assembled an inner circle of men and women of extraordinary practical talent.**

his New Deal policies. Congress, appalled by the arrogance of the move, killed the bill.

Despite some truly remarkable achievements—such as the first federally guaranteed minimum wage and the Social Security Act—it is important not to overestimate the effectiveness of the New Deal. Roosevelt did not end the Great Depression—the war did, by reenergizing the economy and mobilizing the nation. But Roosevelt was able to capitalize on the New Deal's success as if it had. It wasn't just a public relations move; it was an important step in staving off the kind of revolutionary fervor—often masking totalitarian intentions—that was sweeping Europe. By the beginning of 1939 the threats of Hitler and Japan led the President to shrewdly declare that the New Deal was a success: "As a nation, we have rejected any radical, revolutionary programs."[20] This achievement contrasted dramatically with what was happening in parts of Europe and Russia. It was from these regions where the greatest tests of Roosevelt's leadership would come.

Roosevelt could be difficult. He had a short attention span. During the war, his Secretary of the Army, Henry Stimson, complained in his diary that FDR would stay on one subject for only about thirty seconds, but that thirty seconds was generally on target. Roosevelt was strong because he knew his weaknesses. He was a poor manager, so he assembled an inner circle of men and women of extraordinary practical talent. In doing so, he made his weakness his strength—he knew he needed great counsel.

> When the Nazis provoked war with Europe in 1938, President Roosevelt said, "I've been Dr. 'New Deal.' Now I'm Dr. 'Win the War.' "

A sailor and a former Assistant Secretary of the Navy, Roosevelt knew how to change course. When the Nazis provoked war with Europe in 1938, he moved from a partisan-fueled New Deal strategy to a bipartisan one designed to bring the nation together. As he said to leading New Dealer Harry Hopkins, "I've been Dr. 'New Deal.' Now I'm Dr. 'Win the War.'" Hopkins replied, "To Hell with the 'New Deal.' I'm your man to win the war." FDR saw that the danger posed by the Nazis was infinitely greater than the danger posed by party politics at home.[21]

For all his foresight, however, there is evidence that the Roosevelt administration—like that of George W. Bush, half a century later—misinterpreted available intelligence in the run up to Pearl Harbor, as illustrated in Roberta Wohlstetter's book, *Pearl Harbor: Warning and Decision*.[22] There were clear signals throughout 1941 of the coming Japanese attack, which were rejected in Washington on the basis that an attack on British or Dutch colonies in East Asia would be far more in line with Japanese interests than an assault on Pearl Harbor. In other words, it was believed that the potential enemy would reason as we did. In this case, Roosevelt's advisers failed him.

Still, more often, they rose to the occasion. Roosevelt was imperious and did not usually take contradictions well. But he knew when to let those with more expertise speak. In early 1938, when Brigadier General George C. Marshall first met with the President and other senior Cabinet members, Marshall told the President that his strategy to invest most of the defense budget on 15,000 bombers to deter Hitler was flawed. General Marshall insisted that air, ground, and sea forces would be needed in balanced proportion. All present thought that Marshall's career had just ended.

But Roosevelt was impressed and soon made George Marshall Army Chief of Staff. It is a tribute to Roosevelt that he wanted Marshall at his side to tell him when he was truly wrong. Marshall turned out to be the crucial figure in the war, because, as FDR foresaw, he knew how to plan and mobilize.

FDR was one of the greatest Presidential "mobilizers," and the next President should study his example in view of our recent failures in this area. He organized the government to work in unison, and then drew on all elements of the private sector: business, manufacturing, scientific research, education, and medicine. He saw how important scientific research, especially, would be to the war effort. At the war's end, German Admiral Karl Doenitz is said to have admitted that the Nazis were defeated by American science. (G.I.s might not agree, but the contributions of American science and industry were decisive at sea and in the air.)

Notoriously, Roosevelt assumed far-reaching Presidential powers during his third and fourth terms. The great Constitutional scholar Edward Corwin noted that by 1945, a "constitution of rights" had become "a constitution of powers" vested in the Chief Executive.[23] FDR cited Lincoln's suspension of habeas corpus and use of martial law as a precedent for the ruthless internment in what amounted to concentration camps for American citizens of Japanese descent. It will always be a blight on Roosevelt's legacy. But other actions that overrode the president's jurisdiction were more effective and ultimately justifiable. Even before the war, in September 1940, Roosevelt directly defied the recently passed Neutrality Act when he gave England use of American destroyers in exchange for rights to British naval bases. He covertly authorized American ships to fire on German ones in the Atlantic, though he did seek Congressional support in what became the Lend-Lease Act, transferring $50 billion in war supplies to allies from 1941 through 1945.

Roosevelt's decisive use of war powers saved England just as Lincoln's had saved the Union. But a warning note to future Presidents should be attached to these legacies: these two great war leaders were fighting total wars, which engaged virtually the entire economy of the United States, and demanded of the

American people profound sacrifice—a state of affairs we have not seen since 1945. The course they took should never be followed lightly. FDR asked for sacrifice on the part of the American people, but he also spoke with compassion. He battled polio, the Great Depression, and tyranny. It is no wonder that even Ronald Reagan boasted of voting four times for FDR, whom he called our greatest President in modern times.[24]

Harry Truman: Mobilizer for the Cold War

Until Franklin Roosevelt's sudden death in mid-April 1945, Vice President Harry S. Truman knew little of what FDR was doing. Shortly before meeting with his new compatriots in England and the Soviet Union, Truman was informed for the first time of the "Manhattan Project"—a dash to create the atomic bomb that would end World War II in a matter of months. At Potsdam, he met with Joseph Stalin and Winston Churchill without fully knowing what they and FDR had decided in the past.

A plain-spoken man from Missouri, Harry Truman was no genius. But he had practical skills and historical sensibility that allowed him to develop an extraordinary national security team. Like FDR in the Second World War, Truman believed that institutions would be the basic mechanism for winning the Cold War. The Marshall Plan, the National Security Council (NSC), the Central Intelligence Agency, the Defense Department, the North Atlantic Treaty Organization (NATO), and the National Science Foundation (NSF) all came into existence during his tenure. The NSF was the final legacy of the brilliant scientist and engineer, Vannevar Bush, whose role in the Second World War is highlighted in Part II. His postwar contribution was a 1945 report entitled *Science—the Endless Frontier*, which called for public support for university research— a critical dimension of national strength that continues into our time. Though Bush wanted an NSF even more powerful than Truman was willing to create, this transparent grant-making foundation has nevertheless been consistently rated as the most efficient government-related organization.[25]

In the 1946 midterm elections, President Truman lost both Houses of Congress. Starving Europe was in chaos, and Communism was on the march. When the State Department Policy Planning Council came up with a plan for the reconstruction of Europe, in light of his low polls Truman in effect said, "Don't put my name on it." Instead he put George Marshall's name on the plan, and directed him to negotiate with Republican Senator Arthur Vandenberg to obtain his suggestions and assent. Against all odds, the result was one of the greatest legislative and diplomatic successes in American history: the Marshall Plan.

Marshall, working with General Dwight Eisenhower, also put his stamp on the National Security Act of 1947. This Act created the NSC, a sounding-board for the President in foreign policy decision-making, comprised originally of the Vice President, the Secretaries of State and Defense, and later enlarged to include other advisors. Amendments in 1949 established the modern Department of Defense. These institutions still provide Presidents with an indispensable framework for devising, critiquing, and honing foreign policy, as well as building interagency cooperation and public-private partnerships. When Presidents have tried to circumvent the NSC process—such as Kennedy in authorizing the Bay of Pigs invasion, Reagan in sanctioning arms-for-hostages trading with Iran, and George W. Bush in the run-up to the Iraq War—the results have been disastrous.

Truman left a strong legacy of government reform. In many of his initiatives, he saw how important it was to draw on the experiences and talent of a range of people, whatever their political identity. Stressing bipartisanship, he brought in former Republican President Herbert Hoover to set up a series of task forces in 1947 to reform government, which would later be known as the Hoover Commissions. Faced with the current diversity of challenges—as we shall see in the next part of this book—the next President would do well to establish his or her own version of the Hoover Commissions at the very beginning of his or her term.

On June 24, 1950 came a great test for the Truman Administration. North Korea made a surprise assault across the 38th parallel, turning the Cold War hot. The Secretary of State and the Joint Chiefs of Staff had not included South Korea in our stated national security sphere in the Pacific, and for the North Koreans this was an invitation to seize it. But President Truman saw his error. Korea was a dagger pointed at Japan. The decisive Truman went not to the Congress, but to the United Nations in emergency sessions. He calculated that it was an international struggle, not simply a domestic matter, and it would require international support and sanction.

The Security Council made the United States the Executive agent, with UN members providing military forces. President Truman named General Douglas MacArthur as Commander-in-Chief of United Nations Command. Rather than going it alone, the United States benefited from having major allied partners. In 1952, I found myself in Korea as a West Point graduate and a company commander in the 25th Infantry Division. The adjacent brigade in our division was Turkish and was noted for rushing enemy trenches with bayonets. As part of a coalition, I came to appreciate the deep importance of having allies with major troop commitments.

Truman's decision to go to the United Nations instead of Congress had troubling ramifications, however. It reinforced a precedent—begun, as we have seen, with John Adams and the quasi war with France—of undeclared military engagements. Korea set the model for Vietnam and Iraq. While this expansion of Presidential war powers seemed to play to the short-term advantage of the Executive, these undeclared and limited "policy" wars tend to have only short-term public support, and they almost inevitably lack the level of mobilization necessary for complete success. Despite international backing, Truman eventually lost the support of his countrymen in what appeared to be an endless conflict. When he fired the tremendously popular General MacArthur, he saw his popularity plummet to the 20 percent range.

> ∞ **Undeclared and limited "policy" wars tend to have only short-term public support, as they almost inevitably lack the level of mobilization necessary for complete success.**

Despite this sad ending, Truman is almost universally rated in the category of "near great" Presidents due to his solid accomplishments like the Marshall Plan and creation of NATO. Like George Washington, Abraham Lincoln, and Franklin Roosevelt, he understood the importance of creating the institutions for successful leadership. Truman's near greatness has been reinforced by David McCullough's magisterial biography: "As much as any President since Lincoln he brought to the highest office the language and values of the common American people. He held to the old guidelines: work hard, do your best, speak the truth, assume no airs, trust in God, have no fear."[26] As McCullough quotes Eric Severeid, "It's character, just character. He stands like a rock in memory now."*

---

* While MacArthur's "no substitute for victory" was wrongly applied to the Korean War when United Nations forces went beyond the limited measure and brought the Chinese into the war, it is correct in saying that once committed to a war we must organize for success. Failing to articulate clear, limited objectives tends to limit the chances of victory, which has been evident in the Vietnam and Iraq conflicts.

Dwight Eisenhower: Grand Strategist and Institutional Organizer

Like George Washington, Abraham Lincoln, Franklin Roosevelt, and Harry Truman, five-star General and President Dwight D. Eisenhower strongly believed that the key to leadership in war—hot or cold—was organization. He established the position of White House Chief of Staff to the President.* He believed in coordinating all elements of power for success, as demonstrated by his personal experience of marshalling allies to carry out D-Day, the greatest invasion in history. Eisenhower was a great planner, and had a keen awareness of how the best-laid plans can often go awry.

---

* Dwight Eisenhower believed that "organization cannot make a genius out of an incompetent," but, "disorganization can easily lead to disaster." The organizer of Nazi defeat in Europe was also the best organizer of the growing White House staff of any President in the twentieth century. However, he could err in judgment about people. For example: former governor Sherman Adams, his Chief of Staff. Adams was extraordinarily efficient, but his arrogance eventually alienated Members of Congress, valuable campaign contributors, and political allies. These factors, along with ethics issues, resulted in Adam's departure from the White House and replacement by an opposite personality: the humble, retired Major General Jerry Persons, who immediately opened up the White House to people and exposed the President to more diverse sources of information.

Presidents John Kennedy and Lyndon Johnson did not have true Chiefs of Staff and often seemed to enjoy the more ad hoc, sometimes chaotic atmosphere they had learned on Capitol Hill. Richard Nixon went back to the Dwight Eisenhower model with another dominant Chief of Staff, Robert Haldeman. A milder Jack Watson served Jimmy Carter, and in the first Ronald Reagan Administration, a troika reigned: James Baker III, Ed Meese, and Mike Deaver. This resulted in an open White House and served to draw the President into policy discussions.

At the urging of his mentor General George Marshall, Eisenhower conducted a remarkable exercise to test alternative Cold War strategies at the very outset of his Presidency: the so-called Project Solarium, in which three teams of foreign policy experts thoroughly explored and defended rival strategic options. Similarly, Eisenhower transformed the National Security Council by creating a planning council to anticipate emerging threats and opportunities. Eisenhower believed that those concerned with daily operations could not look over and across the horizon to be long-range strategists. Since Eisenhower, no President has ever adopted such a model.

The next President should take a hint from Ike.*

Eisenhower also played an important role in the progress of American efforts in science and engineering. On October 4, 1957, the Soviets launched the first space capsule, Sputnik, shocking Americans who believed that the United States led the way in missile development and space technology. After the initial surprise, the Eisenhower administration used this failure as a catalyst to reenergize American efforts in science education, research, and development. The Sputnik crisis precipitated the creation of NASA, dramatic increases in funding for the NSF, the creation of the Defense Advanced Research Projects Agency (DARPA), and the passage of the National Defense Education Act of 1958. The Act is generally credited with galvanizing the resources that trained a generation of U.S. scientists and engineers.

---

* See Part II, p. 78, for a detailed discussion of Project Solarium. In CSP's 2000 *Comprehensive Strategic Review*, we recommended that the next President establish a similar contingency council to address the evolving and complex threats of today. Had such a council been put into place early in 2001, we may have better anticipated the al-Qaeda attacks and been better prepared to deal with Iraq and Afghanistan.

In 1957, President Eisenhower also created the President's Foreign Intelligence Advisory Board (PFIAB) as a permanent "B" team, so to speak, to monitor and test the quality and assumptions of intelligence.* He staffed it with the best. Unlike some subsequent PFIABs, members were not golf-playing pals, but eminent professionals, such as scientists George Kistakousky, Edwin Land, and William Baker (creator of Bell Laboratories). Eisenhower also formalized the position of Science Advisor to the President and established the United States Information Agency along with the Voice of America. He rightly believed that the contest of ideas was ultimately as important as the conduct of armies.

> ∽ **Eisenhower rightly believed that the contest of ideas was ultimately as important as the conduct of armies.**

In 1956, Eisenhower scored again as a grand strategist, initiating the Federal Interstate and Defense Highway Act. While its primary purpose was to aid national security, Eisenhower had in mind "new highways . . . to get around the country in case of attack," which simultaneously resulted in investment in the future of our economic prosperity. It fostered "urban development, land reclamation, hospital construction, and water conservation." He named a trained engineer, former General Lucius D. Clay, Military Governor in Germany after World War II and "father" of the Berlin airlift—to oversee the initial phase of the vast project.

The Eisenhower initiative, Geoffrey Perret writes in our CSP case studies, "was an extraordinary achievement. The

---

* The Richard Lounsbery Foundation has given a grant supporting a project at Texas A&M University studying all past PFIABs. Roman Popadiuk, Michael Desch, and Michael Absher, *The President's Foreign Intelligence Advisory Board (PFIAB): Learning Lessons from Its Past to Shape Its Future*, due to be published May 2008.

Democrats controlled both the Senate and the House, and his own party—which contained a powerful and vociferous anti-New Deal element—hardly seemed to notice that Eisenhower's highway program amounted to the biggest public works project in American history."[27] It is a reminder for the next President of a good example of an investment in national security *and* national prosperity.

In the study of past Presidents and crisis management, it is instructive to review the next big intervention temptation that was placed before the Commander-in-Chief. Eisenhower had brought the Korean War to an end by what might be called coercive diplomacy. He allowed bombing of dams in North Korea and moved tactical nuclear weapons to the Far East, although there is no indication that he planned to use them. He let his movements be hinted through Indian diplomatic channels as contingencies if the Chinese Communists did not complete the truce negotiations. It worked. Soon after Joseph Stalin's death in March of 1953, the truce was signed on July 27, 1953, as my company was poised to stage a daylight attack. But he did all this with the diplomatic solution in sight. He saw the need for words to be backed up by force—but also for force to be preceded, and, if possible, averted, by words.

Vietnam is a different and perplexing story. There was no clear beginning of our involvement, unlike North Korea's invasion of South Korea. The only abrupt marker was the Dien Bien Phu crisis. In 1954, with the French Foreign Legion losing against the Communists, France had initiated what we might now call "a surge" of their forces, hoping to draw the Communists into open battle. This plan involved committing fresh battalions to an isolated base near the Laotian border, which was soon surrounded by the Communist Vietminh. The French made a major appeal for U.S. intervention, which Secretary of State John Foster Dulles and Joint Chiefs of Staff Chairman Arthur Radford favored.

In response, Eisenhower elucidated five criteria for U.S. intervention:

1. The conflict must be part of a larger concept of Cold War strategy, not just restricted to a single location.
2. Allied support would be crucial.
3. Indigenous support would be crucial.
4. It must have Congressional support.
5. It must have both an entrance and an exit strategy. No President before or since had laid out so clearly the conditions of U.S. intervention. When they were not met, Eisenhower, to the consternation of Dulles and Radford, decided not to intervene.

During the Kennedy-Johnson era, no such clear criteria were ever presented. Nor were such criteria set by George W. Bush before the Iraq intervention. Strategic planning and benchmarks pay historic dividends.

Eisenhower believed in restrained power, avoiding the peaks and valleys of defense spending, so as to maintain a vibrant economy. As a five-star general, who had organized the defeat of Hitler's armies, he had the confidence that came with not having to prove himself, unlike the subsequent three Presidents during the Vietnam conflict. He intervened in the 1956 Lebanon landing conducted by the Sixth Fleet in a swift and limited way.*

---

* Instability of the pro-Western Christian-Muslim Lebanese government was exacerbated by the formation of the pro-Soviet United Arab Republic (UAR) in 1958, which united the countries of Syria and Egypt into a single political entity. When the UAB encouraged similar Arab nationalist coups in Iraq and Jordan, a fearful Lebanese government requested that U.S. troops be brought in to shore up the Administration. A total of 14,357 U.S. soldiers and Marines participated in this expedition, which lasted from July 15 to October 15, 1958, and helped stabilize Lebanon until the mid-1970s.

Following Sputnik, some defense-minded Democrats, led by Senator Henry M. "Scoop" Jackson, fostered the perception of a missile gap. Nowadays, interestingly enough, we would label these liberals "hard-liners." I remember Dick Bolling, a young Democratic Congressman from Missouri, saying to me "time is running out, and we will soon be under Soviet missile superiority. We are reaching the point of maximum danger." Senator Jack Kennedy made this issue his theme, with the implication that golf-playing Ike might not be on top of things.

Here, an exasperated Eisenhower stumbled. He knew the intelligence reports from U-2 spy planes over the Soviet Union had dispelled these fears, but he acted a bit like the great engineer Herbert Hoover, who would not bother to state his case effectively. He treated the intellectual critics as a nuisance. Under the next administration, the new Secretary of Defense Robert McNamara announced that he reviewed the intelligence and that the gap did not exist after all. Even so, Kennedy did move forward on a major missile buildup which some academics say set off a new arms race.

There were also charges of a gap in effective conventional military forces; retired General Maxwell Taylor had called for a reduced nuclear emphasis and a more flexible conventional response at NATO. Here, the critics were correct. Taylor and retired Lieutenant General James Gavin accused Eisenhower of being unwilling to build up conventional forces capability. Eisenhower responded with irritation in his famous Farewell Address, warning against "the military-industrial complex."[28]*

---

* It is interesting to note that whereas the Democratic Party of recent times has been characterized as being weak on defense, the party of Jack Kennedy and Henry "Scoop" Jackson heralded "the time of maximum danger." I remember that at the 1960 Republican National Convention, where I had been asked to be the professional advisor to the national security plank of the party platform, Mel

Eisenhower was regarded by Democratic critics and some Republicans as too detached, and the NSC system as "paper-bound and bureaucratic." But from the work of Professor Fred Greenstein and subsequently revealed White House records, we now know that Eisenhower was the only President in history to meet weekly with his National Security Council. He himself would crisply summarize the decisions reached.[29]

John F. Kennedy: The New Frontier

On January 20, 1961, with a capital covered in snow, forty-three-year-old John Fitzgerald Kennedy delivered his "New Frontier" message. In crafting it, he had his adviser, Theodore Sorensen, study the composition of another famous short address, Abraham Lincoln's speech at Gettysburg. Kennedy's speech, while certainly not the equal of Lincoln's greatest accomplishments, was nonetheless one of the most memorable inaugurals of all time. Kennedy said: "We observe today not as a victory of party but a celebration of freedom. . . . In the long history of the world, only a few generations have been granted that role of defending freedom in its hours of maximum danger."** And those final, famous, stirring lines: "Ask not what your country can do for you, but what you can do for your country."[30] With this statement, a younger generation of Americans was inspired to enter and support public service.

Laird, named the vice-chair of the convention, retorted to me that "the Democrats just want to build up our conventional forces, and get us into a land war again in Southeast Asia." Jackson served as a mentor for such neoconservatives of the future as staffer Richard Perle.

** This young President had, like Theodore Roosevelt and Lincoln, a keen sense of history, having authored both *Profiles in Courage* (New York: Harper, 1956) and *Why England Slept* (New York: W. Funk, Inc., 1940).

That snowy January day, as outgoing Director of the House Republican Policy Committee, I passed the young Congressman Melvin R. Laird (WI), a former Kennedy critic. Mel exclaimed that he had never heard anything quite like JFK's speech. He wasn't alone. Kennedy's eloquent call to win the space race was able to build upon his National Defense Education Action (NDEA), designed to pump funds into universities as well as basic research. Kennedy's pledge to put a man on the moon spawned a new generation of scientists, most of whom are now nearing retirement age and must be replaced by a new generation, lest we lose our competitive edge.

> "Ask not what your country can do for you, but what you can do for your country."
> —John F. Kennedy

But in April 1961, from his high-wire leadership heights, he fell into the Bay of Pigs. It serves to remind the next President how quickly a grand entrance can be followed by a bad stumble. This one came about partly because Kennedy had discontinued the Eisenhower NSC staff planning system, committing the same failure that was to plague Reagan during the Iran-Contra scandal and George W. Bush during the Iraq War. Eisenhower's system had its flaws and critics, but it was the foundation of an important policy, emphasizing planning and organization. Kennedy, a kind of maverick, disregarded his predecessor's policy at his peril.

By October 1962, however, Kennedy had fully restored his leadership with his masterful handling of the Cuban Missile Crisis. He corrected the organizational errors of the Bay of Pigs by establishing an Executive Committee for crisis management (EXCOMM). He required his associates to read Barbara Tuchman's *Guns of August*, describing how miscalculations produced World War I.[31] With such lessons, he ultimately offered Nikita Khrushchev a way out of the missile crisis by giving him written assurance that we would not invade Cuba, and furthermore agreed to the removal of U.S. missiles from Turkey. Through it all, he showed strength and determination as the back-drop of a massive U.S. military alert. Like President Eisenhower, Kennedy learned to exercise both power and restraint. In August of 1963, he sent the first arms control agreement with the Soviet Union to the Senate for ratification.

Kennedy had strengthened himself with a bipartisan Cabinet, enlisting Wall Street banker and Republican Douglas Dillon as Secretary of Treasury and Republican John McCone as CIA director. Kennedy understood the importance of reaching out to gain the public's trust. When he stumbled, he was mature and politically shrewd to assume full responsibility quickly and completely, not incrementally. The master strategist Napoleon said, "In war, everyone makes mistakes; it is he who makes the fewest who wins." We might add, "and he who learns more from his mistakes."*

---

* A major turning point in Americanizing the Vietnam War occurred on October 1 and 2, 1963, when the Kennedy Administration concurred in the military coup in Saigon to overthrow Ngo Dinh Diem with the unintended consequence of his murder. This fatal decision for regime change was made without thorough National Security Council staffing, but like our overthrow of Saddam Hussein, gave our nation ownership for what followed. "When you break the pottery you own it," Colin Powell warned Bush about the invasion of Iraq. It is interesting that it was Vice President Lyndon Johnson who felt our complicity in regime change was a grave mistake. Ironically, within two months he was to inherit the consequence. The other option besides regime change would have been to back away from Vietnam and concentrate on strengthening the SEATO alliance, focusing our center of gravity in Thailand. Two sources that are especially informative on the subject are David Halberstam's *The Best and the Brightest* (New York: Random House, 1969, pp. 286–23) and Fredrik Logevall's *Choosing War: The Lost Chance for Peace and the Escalation of War in Vietnam* (Berkeley: University of California Press, 1999, pp. 34–42).

Lyndon Johnson: Triumph at Home, Failure in Vietnam

Then came John Kennedy's assassination on November 22, 1963 and the Texan Lyndon Baines Johnson was elevated to the Presidency. He was no media darling, but he had truly remarkable legislative abilities.* Cajoling Members of Congress and even managing legislative relations for Executive departments, he oversaw the passage of the Civil Rights Act of 1964 and the creation of Volunteers In Service to America (VISTA), the Job Corps, and Head Start. The Twenty-fourth Amendment ratified under his Presidency, eliminated poll taxes. These were his finest achievements, and they were accomplished despite the opposition of a conservative coalition of fellow southern Democrats.

Johnson skillfully named Democratic and Republican conferees who appealed to minority constituents. He made Senator Everett McKinley Dirksen of Illinois a full partner in his civil rights initiative, and, in turn, Dirksen delivered twenty-nine of the thirty-five Republican votes for the bill, a higher percentage than Vice President Hubert Humphrey managed to assemble amongst the Democrats. It was a genuine coming together across the aisle. The following May, Johnson offered his full vision of the Great Society. In 1965, he succeeded in passing the Voting Rights Act, requiring standard voter registration tests and enabling the federal government to register voters where states had failed to include these registration capabilities.

If George Washington, James Madison, and Alexander Hamilton had been thoroughly republican, Lyndon Johnson had now instilled in our government something thoroughly

---

*As Michael Beschloss noted in his CSP case study on Lyndon Johnson's first one hundred days in office, Johnson established fourteen task forces on urgent issues of the time. He wanted to be known as "a frugal centrist rather than a big spending champion of big government." Beschloss identified Johnson's six keys to success: conviction, timing, personnel, legislative skills, bully pulpit, and flexibility.

democratic. This had been accomplished by extraordinary political skills and political courage. There would be a cost Johnson recognized: eventual loss of much of the south to the Republican Party. The sacrifice should have placed him among the "near great" Presidents, had it not been for the tragedy of Vietnam. Johnson succeeded superbly on the domestic scene, but stumbled over his inherited war in Vietnam. In the wake of a reported North Vietnamese torpedo attack on American destroyers, Congress passed the Gulf of Tonkin Resolution, 410-0 in the House and 88-2 in the Senate, granting the President authority "to take all necessary steps including use of armed force" to protect American interests in Southeast Asia. Johnson had effectively initiated war without a declaration. He did not want to be remembered as the President who lost Vietnam, but he could not bring himself to call for changes in Pentagon leadership and the public sacrifices needed to win. He placed his fate in the hands of a brilliant but misguided Secretary of Defense, Robert McNamara, and the experienced General William Westmoreland. They had a deeply flawed strategy of waging attrition warfare, with incremental troop increases reaching half a million men. Their scientific-seeming "body count" strategy sounded smart in briefings with the President, while the army's "kill ratios" and "search and destroy" tactics impressed outsiders. But they masked a deteriorating situation.

In 1968, the communist Tet Offensive reached the walls of Saigon and broke the Administration's will to continue the fight in Washington and provide Westmoreland with his requested troop increases. As would be the case almost forty years later, the President was allowed, and even encouraged, to state repeatedly that light was at the end of the tunnel. Johnson's skittishness about the war and his desire to minimize it was apparent in his January 1966 State of the Union message, in which he gave equal weight to his wartime and peacetime objectives. As Americans were dying overseas, Johnson seemed loathe to give priority to the war issue and mobilize the country. Even his Treasury Secretary, Henry Fowler, did not fully know how Johnson intended to pay for the war. Decisions on national security were made over "Tuesday lunches," not through a NSC decision-making process. LBJ's skills, which were so clearly evident on the domestic front, deserted him in dealing with Vietnam. In 1968, he withdrew from the Presidential race and left office a broken man, in spite of his magnificent domestic legacy.

Richard Nixon: From Brilliance to Disaster

Unfortunately, Richard Nixon's legacy will always be overshadowed by his ignominious departure from office. But before the Watergate scandal broke, he had many accomplishments to his credit. Before he was inaugurated as President, he reformed the office of Vice President, turning it from a largely ceremonial position into a more active, robust role, traveling the world and running commissions for Eisenhower. In 1968, he campaigned with the promise that he had "a plan to end the war and win the peace." In 1969, he announced the Guam doctrine, which stated that security problems should be handled by Asians themselves along with our support, and he soon announced the withdrawal of 25,000 troops from Vietnam. Attrition warfare, search and destroy, and body counts were replaced by "Vietnamization," transferring the struggle from American troops to the South Vietnamese. For the most part, Nixon was smart and effective in conducting foreign affairs. He and National Security Advisor Henry Kissinger pulled off diplomatic coups by opening diplomatic relations with China and seeking détente with the Soviet Union, while working to isolate both powers from North Vietnam.

On the home front, Nixon showed great interest in pursuing government reform. He asked Roy Ash, former head of Litton

Industries, to set up a Presidential Advisory Council on Executive Organization (later known as the Ash Commission), to promote a results-oriented approach to government leadership. Out of this came the Office of Management and Budget (OMB), the Environmental Protection Agency (EPA), the Occupational Safety and Health Administration (OSHA), and the National Oceanic and Atmospheric Administration (NOAA).

The formation of the EPA is particularly instructive. To pull off this bold and controversial move, Nixon worked deftly with Democrats in Congress, with his legislative office headed by Congressional liaison Bill Timmons. Opposition from special interest groups was very strong, but ultimately many figures from both parties supported this proposal for a focused agency with strong interdepartmental crosswalks. Nixon is not generally remembered for his domestic agendas or Congressional outreach, but his founding of the EPA and the popular New Federalism programs are models of how to accomplish directives through building coalitions. Strangely, even Nixon failed to mention these exemplary achievements in his memoirs.

> A President cannot lead without trust, for the nation will not unite behind him or her without it.

The man who had vowed to "end the war" blundered in the spring of 1970, when he sought to take out enemy bases from the Cambodian sanctuaries from which our troops were attacked. Nixon did this without alerting any member of Congress. Even though it was intended to be temporary, this unannounced escalation of the war went against Nixon's campaign pledge to start military withdrawals with a new strategy of Vietnamization. It shocked Congress and the nation, and reactivated the antiwar movement on campuses. Senators Frank Church (ID) and John Sherman Cooper (KY) passed an amendment codifying the temporary nature of the move, as well as restricting the President's power to authorize further ground operations into Cambodia and preventing air strikes not directly aimed at protecting our troops.[*] The exit from Vietnam was messy and complicated, and the way in which it was implemented could have been avoided.[32] It has been much examined in recent months, as historians and military tacticians alike have searched for a way out of the morass in Iraq. While the Vietnam situation was notably different from the one before us today, it is still worth noting the chain of events. General Creighton Abrams Jr. shared tentative dates for troop withdrawals with the South Vietnamese leadership to show them that the government was serious about a pullout—and to urge them to stand up as we stood down. As Assistant Secretary of State in late 1970, I visited South Vietnam and saw notable success. In 1972, during the so-called Easter Offensive of the North Vietnamese, South Vietnamese forces carried their own, with the aid of our air power and advisors. At that point, their capabilities were far ahead of the indigenous Iraqi forces today. By early 1973, the Paris Peace Accord was signed, which began the withdrawal of troops, returned our prisoners of war, and put the South Vietnamese in charge of fighting and negotiating with the North.

This is somewhat similar to the December 2006 recommendations of the Iraq Study Group's new strategy for Iraq—but the

_____

[*] At the time, I was brought in as Assistant Secretary of State for Congressional Relations, with the job of repairing the broken political relationship between the Senate and the White House. We were able to negotiate a modification of the Cooper-Church Amendment with the authors, which allowed limited air strikes in Cambodia, if needed, to protect our troops in Vietnam. It is interesting that in the Lam Son Offensive into Laos six months later, we were able to persuade the White House to have us inform key people on the Hill in advance. The secret was kept by the members of Congress and none of the members commented on our airpower in support of the Vietnamese operation, until it was over.

situation with respect to the Iraqi leadership has deteriorated so much even from the time of the Study Group's recommendations that it would be difficult for their forces to assume the same role that the South Vietnamese did thirty-five years ago. Late in 1973 and 1974, everything changed, in Vietnam and at home. With the revelation of the Watergate break-in, trust in the President was devastated. The lesson cannot be stated strongly enough—a President, particularly during a time of war, cannot lead without trust, for the nation will not unite behind him or her. A disillusioned Congress steadily cut funds and withdrew political support. A series of Congressional amendments cut support for the war as the Communists stepped up attacks. Congressional leaders so mistrusted Watergate-riddled Nixon that they feared he would reinvolve the United States in a new war in Vietnam and Cambodia.[*]

---

[*] Richard Nixon was forced to make a televised statement about Watergate on April 29, 1974. The controversy over Watergate was soon matched by controversy over a report of the Senate Foreign Relations Committee about U.S. bombing in Cambodia, which was in violation of the 1971 Cooper-Church Amendment (the modification of the original amendment I had negotiated with the authors to allow for bombing only when our troops were being fired upon from Cambodian sanctuaries). By May, there were an increasing number of Senators switching their support of the war. By June, there was a cut-off amendment introduced, that denied further funding for military activities in Southeast Asia after August 15. Our last P.O.W. was returned on March 29, 1973, ending our direct military participation in the second Indochina War.

In the other part of the Congressional revolt, there was enacted the War Powers Act of 1973. The original, stricter Senate version was watered down by the House, but even with the Republican Leader Gerald Ford favoring some restriction. The bill set a limit of sixty days for Presidential use of force that was not approved of by Congress, with an additional thirty days to withdraw those forces.

Nixon's downfall was due in no small part to the culture of secrecy he cultivated. Its lethal effects were evident well before the Watergate break-in. In August of 1971, a group of Nixon aides and former intelligence officers hatched a plan to break into the office of the psychiatrist of Daniel Ellsberg, the former State- and Defense-Department analyst who had authored and leaked the Pentagon Papers, which revealed secret operations and duplicitous behavior on the part of the Johnson administration in Vietnam. Even though Ellsberg worked for the previous administration, Nixon's circle thought he needed to be discredited. A leak was something to be stopped at almost any cost. And so were born the White House "plumbers," who were later used to break into the Democratic Headquarters.

Among this group was a young Deputy Assistant to the President, Egil Krogh, who wrote in the *New York Times* that "the premise of our action was the strongly held view within certain precincts of the White House that the President . . . could carry out illegal acts with impunity if they were convinced that the nation's security demanded it." In 2001, shortly after George W. Bush's inauguration, Krogh wrote a letter to the new President's staff, particularly his lawyers: "I said that integrity required them to constantly ask, is it legal? And I recommended that they

∞ **Nixon's downfall was due in no small part to the culture of secrecy he cultivated.**

There was not a sufficient House vote to override a veto. However, this situation changed dramatically on October 20, 1973 with the so-called Nixon Saturday Night Massacre, opening the second stage of Watergate, and producing an override of the President's veto on November 7, 1973. In other words, lack of Presidential trust lead to the enactment of the War Powers Bill.

rely on well-established legal precedent and not some hazy, loose notion of what phrases like 'national security' and 'commander in chief' could be tortured into meaning."[33] Daniel Patrick Moynihan served in the first Nixon Administration, and his last book entitled *Secrecy: The American Experience* is another such warning.[34] Wise words for the incoming White House staff, too.

Gerald Ford and Jimmy Carter: Honest, Transitional Presidents

The new President, Gerald Ford, was determined to move both Watergate and Vietnam off the national agenda. In the days that followed his accession to the Presidency, Ford was besieged with questions about his disgraced predecessor. Was Ford going to pardon Nixon for his role in covering up the Watergate scandal? What was he going to do about the incriminating evidence on Nixon's tapes? The idea of a pardon had been planted in Ford's mind by White House Chief of Staff Alexander Haig, but Ford equivocated, leaving the impression at his first news conference that he would wait until the justice system had worked its will. In fact, he quickly decided he had to pardon Nixon immediately, absolving him of all federal crimes he might have committed. He saw it as the only way to get this "long national nightmare" behind him.

Unfortunately for Ford, Nixon did not want to accept a pardon if it meant confessing to his crimes. He grudgingly agreed to take one with a pallid statement regretting his failure to act "more decisively and more forthrightly in dealing with Watergate." Ford took comfort in a 1915 Supreme Court decision his aides had unearthed, saying that acceptance of a pardon was a confession of guilt, but he erred in failing to make that point publicly. However well motivated his desire to put the scandal behind the country, it backfired, and he left himself open to charges that he had made "a deal" with Nixon in order to make himself President. The charges weren't true, but Ford's mishandling of the pardon cost him the election in 1976. Pardons are an issue for any President.[35] But history has absolved Ford, who has won the John F. Kennedy Presidential Library Foundation's Profiles in Courage Award. In retrospect, Ford has been regarded as a great healer after "the long night of Watergate," as a person of great decency, civility, and integrity.

One of the footnotes to the Ford presidency would later affect the conduct of the George W. Bush administration. When Ford came into office, former Congressman Donald Rumsfeld was brought back from his post as Ambassador to NATO to be Ford's Chief of Staff, and Rumsfeld selected Dick Cheney to be his deputy. These two able young men misread the tragedy of defeat in Vietnam. They watched President Ford, powerless to deter the twenty-division North Vietnamese attack in the face of far-reaching Congressional restrictions on providing security support to South Vietnam. Rumsfeld and Cheney saw this as an unconscionable forfeiture of the President's war powers. They, like Kissinger, wanted the President to address a joint session of Congress and, as Ford wrote in his memoir, "tell the American people that Congress was solely to blame for the debacle in Southeast Asia."[36]

Ford did not think this was the right approach. Instead, in communication to Congress, he concluded: "Let us put an end to self-inflicted wounds. Let us remember that our national unity is a most priceless asset. Let us deny our adversaries the satisfaction of using Vietnam to pit Americans against Americans. At this moment the United States must present to the world a united front."[37] The different, and wrong, interpretations of young Cheney and Rumsfeld came back to haunt the George W. Bush Administration, thirty-five years later. The mistakes of the Bush Administration rhyme with those of the Johnson and Nixon Administrations.

The Vietnam experience was filled with tragedy, both in this country and Southeast Asia. As Ford sought to heal our self-inflicted wounds, he also moved dramatically to open America's borders to South Vietnamese refugees who had given their services or support to the American cause. In 1975 alone, more than 125,000 South Vietnamese were permitted to resettle in the United States. Furthermore, over an eight-year period (1975-1982) more than 375,000 relocated throughout our country along with approximately 125,000 Laotians. Compared to these efforts, our refugee policy toward Iraq today has been a dismal failure.

Out of two million current Iraqi refugees only 719 have been admitted into the United States in the current budget year, which runs from October to September, 30 2007.* Contingency planning within the Executive and Legislative branches is not being done to confront the magnitude of what appears to be an emerging refugee crisis over the next couple of years.

Hopefully the new President will follow Ford's example of generosity.

In domestic policy, President Ford had to work with an overwhelmingly Democratic Congress, elected in 1974 as a reaction to Watergate. The president preached fiscal discipline and often wielded his veto pen in its defense. Nevertheless, domestic spending grew much faster than the economy during his brief presidency.

In his 1976 campaign statement Jimmy Carter said, "I'm Jimmy Carter and I'm running for President. I will never lie to you." In a 1982 interview, looking back, he said: "I had a dif-

---

* An estimated 50,000 Iraqis are fleeting their war-ravaged country per month, contributing to the fastest growing refugee population in the world. Matthew Lee, "US Admissions of Iraqi Refugees Rise," *Associated Press,* September 4, 2007.

ferent way of governing, I think, than had been the case with my predecessors. . . . As an engineer and as a Governor I was much more inclined to move rapidly and without equivocation and without the long, interminable consultations and so forth that are inherent, I think, in someone who has a more legislative attitude, or psyche, or training, or experience."[38] He, like Ronald Reagan after him, ran as an outsider, positioning himself against the Establishment. In Carter's case, this turned out to be a failing. It alienated him from many public servants with whom he had to work closely. He even ignored his own party's leader in Congress, Speaker Tip O'Neill. Those who had been slighted were ready to condemn him when he faltered. With Carter's high standard of public morality, noble pronounce-

~ **Carter personally negotiated an Israeli and Egyptian peace.**

ments and placement of human rights on the global agenda, he was hurt by ethical lapses of his own staff, such as the illicit banking practices of his budget director, Burt Lance.

Carter's brilliant National Security Advisor Zbigniew Brzezinski later wrote, "He was trusted, but, unfairly, that trust was in him as a person and not as a leader. . . . His personal qualities—honesty, integrity, religious connections, compassion— were not translated in the public mind into statesmanship with a historical sweep."[39] Like Herbert Hoover, another President who had an easier time focusing on details than articulating a grand vision of the country, he could not communicate effectively, and he failed to gain the love or loyalty of the broader public. (This has changed since he exited office and assumed a prominent role, through the fine Carter Center in Atlanta; he has had an important role tackling poverty and conflict around the world.)

Jimmy Carter's innate command of detail in personal encounters, however, made for a truly great achievement: for two weeks in September 1978, Carter personally negotiated the peace agreement between Egypt's Anwar Al Sadat and Israel's Menachem Begin, ending their state of war and working toward the return of Sinai Peninsula to Egypt. Carter had put his prestige on the line against strong advice to the contrary and produced a major diplomatic breakthrough.

But success did not carry forward. Where many Presidents have failed due to hubris, Carter suffered from excessive timidity.

When Carter's polls dropped, he assembled over 150 political and intellectual American leaders at Camp David to discuss the crisis of confidence and the malaise affecting the country. It was the prelude to firing four prominent members of his Cabinet. Still, already suffering from the 1978-1979 oil crisis and double-digit inflation, on November 5, 1980, the final blow to his Presidency came when Iranian students invaded the American Embassy, taking 52 Americans hostage and holding them for 400 days. The Carter Administration never recovered.

Fred Greenstein appropriately wrote of Carter's political failure:

> His actions provide future Presidents with a multitude of cautions. A President who studied the Carter experience would be alert to the dangers of raising unrealistic expectations, failing to build bridges to Capitol Hill and overloading the national policy agenda.[40]

Ronald Reagan: Uniting at Home and Abroad

There could hardly be two more drastically different White House occupants than outgoing Jimmy Carter and incoming Ronald Reagan. Carter focused intensely on detail; Reagan, not at all. But Reagan was a great communicator, persuader, and visionary. He exuded optimism, and managed to capture the imagination even of those who disagreed with his policies. Announcing that the suffering economy had "come to a turning point," he made it his top priority to build a broad consensus in Congress and the nation to push radical economic reforms. As professor James McGregor Burns wrote,

> Like FDR, Reagan considered himself President of all the people. He designed his inaugural address to reassure Americans that he could pull the country through. Like FDR, he wanted to move quickly on sweeping legislation, to revive the "Hundred Days" of 1933.[41]

The Reagan I came to know is different than the image propagated by some of his ideological followers. I had met him only once during his time as governor, but William French Smith (later named Reagan's Attorney General) told me, "Dave, you should get to know Reagan. He has a constant political philosophy but is not an ideologue." I talked with him early in the campaign at a dinner hosted by George Will to help Reagan avoid Carter's mistake of not connecting with prominent Washingtonians. Host George Will invited people from across the spectrum, including liberal Kay Graham, owner of the *Washington Post*, conservative Democrat Jeane Kirkpatrick, and labor leader Lane Kirkland.

Reagan ran as a Washington outsider, but he warmed to Washingtonians immediately upon his arrival. Nancy Reagan did even more so, and became a second set of eyes and ears for the President, as Eleanor Roosevelt had been for Franklin Roosevelt. Where Eleanor Roosevelt traveled around the country, ingratiating herself into communities of the dispossessed, Nancy traveled among insiders—liberal and conservative alike. She formed deep relationships with important people on both sides of the aisle, giving her great advantages as an aide to her husband.

The beginning of Reagan's Administration was notable for its discipline. Aided by Chief of Staff James Baker's firm attention to details; Edwin Meese, his counselor; Mike Deaver, his idea man; and David Gergen, his communications advisor, the White House quietly shelved the more controversial social issues. The economic crisis inherited from Carter became Reagan's "first, second, and third priority." On a political level, Reagan charmed Southern Democrats and even brought some blue-collar workers into his fold.

In 1983, the Social Security system was in danger of insolvency, and a stalemate arose between Congress and President Reagan. But Reagan broke out of this impasse by calling for an independent National Commission on Social Security, chaired by Alan Greenspan and appointed by the Congress and the President. Speaker Tip O'Neill also supported the measure. As Congressional Budget Director Rudy Penner later wrote, the Democrats "set aside ideological differences in pursuit of pragmatic differences."[42] In utilizing an independent Commission, Reagan availed himself of one of the President's most powerful tools of leadership, as we will discuss toward the end of this section.

> ∿ **Nancy Reagan became a second set of eyes and ears for the President.**

A year and a half into his first term, Reagan dealt with his first military intervention. After the Marine barracks in Beirut were destroyed by a suicide truck bomb on October 23, 1983, killing 242 Marines and sailors, Reagan immediately reviewed the entire U.S. policy in Lebanon. Secretary of State George Shultz, a former Marine, wanted to stay, in order to show our determination. Secretary of Defense Caspar Weinberger wanted to retreat. As some like to tell the story, Reagan said, "Retreat, hell, we will redeploy to the sea." Reagan, like Dwight Eisenhower in 1954, recognized that without significant reinforcement—which it would have been unwise to commit—leaving our troops to fight an insurgency was untenable and dangerous. Wise strategists know when to stay and dig in and when to "redeploy."

In one significant episode, Reagan and his aides were too bold. Like Franklin Roosevelt, Reagan was a poor manager, so he left details to others. This left Reagan dependent—sometimes with ugly results, as in the Iran-Contra Affair. Roosevelt never had such a staff breakdown because FDR had a deep curiosity about his subordinates, which Reagan notoriously lacked. Reagan either took them for granted or simply assumed that they would live up to expectations.

Don Regan, Reagan's second Chief of Staff, had been a successful corporate CEO and Treasury Secretary, but he was too autocratic to be an effective Chief of Staff. He encouraged the image of Prime Minister, with White House operations totally under his direction. When Iran-Contra broke out, however, he disclaimed responsibility. But Reagan himself didn't. As President John Kennedy had with the Bay of Pigs, Reagan fell into a hole over the Iran-Contra affair and, at first, dug in deeper. But after his initial intransigence, he did what good leaders do. He looked for a way out.

On the day after Christmas, 1986, the President phoned me in Brussels (I was Ambassador to NATO at the time). He asked me to come in to the White House for three months as a member of the Cabinet. I would report only to Reagan, bypassing the controversial Chief of Staff Don Regan, to coordinate the Administration's response to the investigation and ensure that integrity was restored to the White House. Reagan told me himself that there would be no executive privilege, an extraordinary position in view of the 3,000 scandal-related documents the FBI had already pulled from NSC files. One of my roles was "to get everything out" to ensure no cover-ups and restore trust in the White House. Shortly before, he had set up a special board including former Senator John Tower of Texas, former Senator Edmund Muskie of Maine, and former NSC Advisor General Brent Scowcroft, to review and report on the flawed process that led to the breakdown and make recommendations for an improved and more accountable NSC process.[43]*

Reagan's decision not to insulate himself in a bubble of denial stood in direct contrast to the actions of Richard Nixon during Watergate. Nixon had been unaware of the Watergate break-in, but he himself led the attempt to cover it up, setting in motion the events that would go on for more than fourteen months and ultimately lead to his resignation under threat of impeachment. He destroyed the credibility of his Presidency, despite extraordinary diplomatic openings to Communist China and the Soviet Union. Reagan, on the other hand, moved quickly, ensured that the process was transparent and was able to recover.

Reagan wanted to end the Cold War and lift the specter of nuclear war from the world. His strong rhetoric—denouncing

---

* Part of my role was to coordinate with Judge Lawrence Walsh, the independent Counsel, who became convinced after my first visit accompanied by my deputy, Judge Charles Brower, that we had put the investigative process in order, therefore saying he would not issue subpoenas. Second, my role was to coordinate with the Congressional investigating committees, and in our three month tenure, we found remarkable bipartisan support and concern that we not lose another President at this particular point in the Cold War. It is interesting to note that in their report the ranking minority Congressman at that time, Dick Cheney, said that Reagan had made a mistake "when he acceded too readily and too completely to waive executive privilege for our committees' investigation." What the Cheney report missed was that by temporarily giving up the precious Presidential asset of executive privilege, rather than diminishing the Presidential power, Reagan restored that power which he had been rapidly losing in this crisis. The complete story is in my book *Saving the Reagan Presidency* (College Station: Texas A & M University Press, 2005.

the "Evil Empire" before a White House prayer breakfast with evangelical Christians, for instance—gave him a hard-line image unpopular in Europe, which was magnified by his determination to use intermediate-range missiles to match the Soviet SS-20s (even though this plan was one of a multilateral alliance initially driven by the European alliance members). In reality, he set up a situation of negotiating from strength. It

> It was Reagan's humility that enabled him to unite much of America and the West and lead us toward the quiet end of the Cold War.

paid off, and he achieved one of the most dramatic diplomatic reversals in our history at his 1985 Geneva summit meeting with Mikhail Gorbachev. Reagan's handlers intended to leave him alone with Gorbachev only for a few minutes of greetings. But Reagan extended his bilateral talk for over an hour. In Gorbachev, Reagan "read" a man in trouble, who might become a partner in bringing the Cold War to an end.

Reagan abhorred the NATO nuclear strategy of "Mutually Assured Destruction" (MAD). To him it was a form of mutual suicide, "a reckless gamble conducive to miscalculation." He seized upon the Strategic Defense Initiative (SDI) as a way out of the nuclear trap. He also saw it as a technological revolution, which the Soviets could not match.

As NATO Ambassador in 1984, I saw his reasoning firsthand. In a meeting with then NATO Secretary General Lord Peter Carrington and the President in the Oval Office, Carrington protested that SDI would be provocative. Reagan responded that when we have developed these defensive technologies we would offer to make them available to the Soviets, that is, Mutually Assured Defense for Mutually Assured Destruction. Sitting next to me, Secretary Weinberger steadied himself from falling off his chair.

This conversation about the MAD strategy eliminating nuclear weapons illustrates how Reagan's mind worked. Like Franklin Delano Roosevelt, his visionary leadership made up for his weaknesses as a manager. Whether or not SDI would have worked exactly as Reagan envisioned, it confirmed to the Soviets that they could not keep up with the technological revolution. Reagan knew himself. He thought he was a man of great ideas, but not a great man, and here he resembled Harry Truman. Reagan possessed a self-deprecating sense of humor. During the Iran-Contra scandal, I had a dozen private meetings with Reagan and I never saw any hint of overweening pride. I believe this characteristic allowed him to get out of the Iran-Contra hole in a way that the more prideful Richard Nixon could never have done.

It was this humility that enabled him to unite much of America and the West and lead us toward the quiet end of the Cold War. And—with the exception of the Iran-Contra episode—he surrounded himself with a few excellent advisors. His Secretary of State, George Shultz, was steady and well organized, able to find practical pathways for Reagan's visions. A Democrat in his younger years, Reagan relied on outstanding Democrats of special abilities: from his Ambassador to Japan, former Democratic Senate Majority Leader Mike Mansfield; his long range strategic weapons negotiator, Humphrey Democrat Max Kampelman; and intermediate range nuclear weapons negotiator Paul Nitze, a Kennedy Democrat. In the early evenings Reagan had Speaker of the House Tip O'Neil over to the White House regularly to swap Irish jokes and to make deals over good whiskey. The two could have not been more opposite in political philosophy, but they saw, as had Rutherford B. Hayes and his U.S. postmaster general Senator David McKendree Key, over a century before, that "He serves his party best who serves his nation."

Domestically, President Reagan showed his flexibility in accepting the reversal of a portion of the very deep tax cuts he had promoted early in his presidency. Nevertheless, the large net tax cuts that remained, together with an acceleration of defense spending, left a large budget deficit that bedeviled his successors.

George H. W. Bush: Military Victory, Political Defeat

George H. W. Bush came to office better prepared than perhaps any other modern President. He had been a Congressman, former Chair of the Republican National Committee, Ambassador to the United Nation, President Nixon's envoy to China, Director of Central Intelligence, Presidential candidate, and Vice President for eight years under a transformational President. He had been an able Vice President, subordinating his agenda to the President's. But as a communicator, he was no Reagan. He waved away the "vision thing" and did not seek to be transformational. His ill-considered pledge: "Read my lips, no new taxes," backfired, and the subsequent shift to fiscal stringency in 1990 was seen as a betrayal. He avoided some of the conservative's favorite social issues without Reagan's finesse, further disaffecting the GOP.

The tax increases in the bipartisan budget agreement of 1990 were highly unpopular, especially with the Republican base. However, those increases and the accompanying spending cuts represented a huge reduction in the budget deficit that was unfortunately obscured in the short run by the recession of 1990. Perhaps more important, the budget deal led to the Budget Enforcement Act of 1990. It required that any tax cut or entitlement increase be paid for with some other tax increase or entitlement cut and it imposed rigid caps on discretionary appropriations and outlays. It disciplined the budget during the remainder of the Bush Administration and was used to good effect by President Bill Clinton in his subsequent battle against the deficit.

George H. W. Bush excelled in the foreign policy arena. He was at ease with his highly skilled Secretary of State James Baker III and trusted National Security Advisor Brent Scowcroft, back for a second term. Bush and Baker did the almost inconceivable at the end of the Cold War when they unified Germany and brought it into the Western Alliance with Moscow's assent. That was transformational. The future of Germany had been the central issue of the Cold War, and Bush managed to solve it masterfully.

> ∾ **Bush and Baker did the almost inconceivable at the end of the Cold War when they unified Germany and brought it into the Western Alliance with Moscow's assent.**

Bush's response to the Iraqi invasion of Kuwait was also deftly handled. He and Baker put together a broad international coalition, which eventually paid for 90 percent of the war's cost. Even Syria contributed a division. To implement their carefully planned strategy, a steady Secretary of Defense Dick Cheney and an organized Chairman of the Joint Chiefs Colin Powell led, while Secretary of State James Baker helped build a coalition of forces. Carefully calculating before the attack, the decision was made to double our forces to half a million, which provided the option of holding the center but creating a brilliant flanking maneuver.

This was quite the opposite of what happened before the current Iraq War, in which the originally proposed forces were cut in half.

One can argue whether the war was stopped three days too soon, when more of Saddam Hussein's Republican Guard could have been trapped. One can also argue about whether the CIA let down the Shiite uprising in Southern Iraq. But overall, the conduct of the elder Bush's Gulf War was clearly America's most successful political-military enterprise since the Second World War, and as effective as any war in American history. To have rushed to Baghdad to unseat Saddam without sufficient planning and preparation would have been even worse than George W. Bush's underplanned invasion and occupation of Iraq. In a way, this would have repeated MacArthur's mistake of pushing beyond his initial objectives and overreaching to the Yalu River, thus bringing Communist China into the Korean War.[*]

George H. W. Bush had an 89 percent poll approval rating at the end of his Gulf War. However, when the nation slipped into an economic recession in 1992, the figure plunged closer to 35 percent. Reagan-conservative Pat Buchanan opened a passionate attack from the Right, and populist Ross Perot jumped in as an independent third party candidate. As a result, in 1992 the elder Bush received only 38 percent of the popular vote, while Bill Clinton received 43 percent, with 19 percent going to Perot. America's center-right conservative majority was fractured less than a decade after Reagan's landslide victories. And yet, Zbignew Brzezinski, who rated the current and past two Presidents, gives George H. W. Bush a foreign policy grade of "B," the highest of the three on global leadership.[**]

---

[*] Furthermore, after the setback to our leadership in the Vietnam War, the Gulf War lifted the morale of the military and the belief that our civilian and military leaders could perform brilliantly. It is appropriate to recall that some of the credit to the victory goes to Carter's Undersecretary of Defense, Bill Perry, who oversaw the development of the advanced technology and weaponry which contributed to victory. Credit goes to General E. C. Meyers, the Army Chief of Staff, who restored to vibrancy a "hollow army" which he had inherited.

[**] Professor Brzezinski denies George H. W. Bush the "A" because he did not build on his German and Kuwait accomplishments to offer a global vision. A tough grader, the Professor gives Clinton a "C" and George W. Bush an "F." Zbignew Brzezinski, *Second Chance* (New York: Basic Books, 2007).

William Clinton: A Visionary, Yet Undisciplined Leader

Bill Clinton had little in common with his Democratic Presidential predecessor, Jimmy Carter, despite the fact that both were former southern Governors. Clinton had charm and charisma to spare; Carter had almost none. But Clinton did repeat the Carter mistakes of initial lack of discipline, erratic priorities, and unclear focus. He became embroiled in debates over homosexuals in the military, which affected relations with the Chairman of the Joint Chiefs of Staff, General Colin Powell, and the Congress.

His failed health care reform proposal by Hillary Clinton is a cautionary tale for Presidents who would impose their will on Congress. As Professor George C. Edwards III writes, it was a daring proposal with "perhaps the most sweeping, complex presumptions for controlling the conduct of state governments, employees, drug manufacturers, doctors, hospitals and individuals, in American history."[44] Sprung on a new Congress in 1994 without sufficient warning or preparation, and without building the necessary coalitions within Congress, the plan was soundly rejected. I believe that Senator Hillary Clinton, in retrospect, would fully agree with this analysis.*

But at other times, Clinton skillfully brought together differing factions. In one instance, the White House was ready to abandon the historic North American Free Trade Agreement

---

* By contrast, David Brooks notes that Senator Hillary Clinton's September 2007 health care plan is "evolutionary, not revolutionary," compared to her previous plan from fourteen years earlier. Her new proposal leaves details to Congress, and clearly states that the "private insurance/employer-base system will still remain the heart and soul of the social contract—it's just that more people will be given tax credits so they can afford to buy in." David Brook, "Hillary Clinton: From Revolution to Evolution," *New York Times*, September 18, 2007: A27.

(NAFTA) for lack of votes in Congress until Clinton brought together establishment figures and lobbyists to achieve an eleventh-hour rescue. Ironically, Jimmy Carter was the figure who helped bring this together (ex-Presidents seem to gain great wisdom). The Carter Center joined with the Center for Strategic and International Studies (which I headed at the time) to form a major commission entitled *NAFTA and Beyond: A New Framework for Doing Business in the Americas.* This blue ribbon commission enlisted an extraordinary array of prominent American leaders including all living Secretaries of State, organized by Henry Kissinger, and was hosted by the President. I watched Clinton's face as he heard from Republicans James Baker and Henry Kissinger and leading Democratic and Republican Congressional figures, who pledged to further the ratification of the NAFTA agreement. A quick learner, Clinton was soon to use the bully pulpit as a proponent of America and globalization, thus going against part of his labor-based Democratic constituency.

With regard to the economy, he had a transforming vision. In this mission, he was aided by a talented Robert Rubin, his economic advisor and subsequent Secretary of Treasury, and his successor Larry Summers, who, like Dwight Eisenhower, felt fiscal solvency was an element of national power. As James Carville put it, "It's the economy, stupid." Clinton said in July 1993:

> Keep in mind the ultimate purpose of deficit reduction is to improve the economy by getting interest rates down, freeing up tax funds that we would otherwise have to spend on servicing the debt, and improving the climate for new jobs. It's also clear that we have to have some investment incentives. People have to take this money we're going to save through reducing the deficit, turn around and invest it in the economy.[45]

In his age of turbulence, Alan Greenspan gave his highest marks to Bill Clinton of the six Presidents he served. Not only for his intellectual grasp of the longer term economic interests of the country but not wavering in that direction due to short-term political interests.

President Clinton and particularly Vice President Gore had great interests in "reinventing government," that is, improving its functionality. Two specific examples are first, the outstanding leadership of the Federal Emergency Management Agency (FEMA) under James Lee Witt.[46] Second, is the initiative under then Vice President Gore to improve the functions and quality of government to include best business practices from the private sector, an effort led by Phil Lader and Elaine Karmack.

Nevertheless, Clinton dropped off in his poll ratings going into the 1994 midterm election and lost the Democratic Congressional majority in the face of Rep. Newt Gingrich's shrewd Contract with America campaign and his 10 Point Conservative Legislative Program. For the first time in forty years, the Republicans controlled both houses of Congress. It was at this point that Clinton worked out his clear strategy of "triangulation," relying on the advice of Dick Morris, who had been a consultant to Republican leaders.[*]

---

[*] Professor James McGregor Burns's latest book, *Walking Alone*, is an admonition for a President to stick firmly to a party line. In a sense, his solution is more for a parliamentary system, which our Founders rejected. He sees some radical movements, coming from the Democratic left, as desirable. His previous coauthored work published during the Clinton Administration, entitled *Dead Center*, condemned Clinton's centrist politics and "triangulation." I disagree with this great scholar, who feels that this is the only way to achieve transformational leadership, the kind of leadership that inspires major reform and upheaval of the status quo. I believe that today successful "movements," whether on the Left or Right, are those that eventually

Not unlike George W. Bush in the days following September 11, 2001, Clinton was helped, politically, by a tragic event. On April 19, 1995, a bomb exploded at the Alfred P. Murrah Federal Office Building in Oklahoma City, killing 163 people. His adept handling of the crisis restored his popularity, and his poll numbers soared to 60 percent. In addition, Speaker of the House Gingrich overreached politically and allowed Clinton to reposition himself as a defender of Social Security, Medicare, education, the environment, the middle class, and even a balanced budget (initially on the GOP agenda). The budget battle then forced the government to shut down, which backfired on Gingrich and the Republicans, and Clinton won the public once again as the "Comeback Kid."** In 1996, Clinton skillfully

---

translate themselves into a modified form of consensus legislation. The civil rights and the environmental movements on the left and the deregulation and tax reform movements on the right are such examples. The pathway for reform movement to party is necessary, but must be pushed beyond party lines to a bipartisan bridge.

** It is a credit to the constructive side of Congress that some wise Republicans and Democrats, working with the White House, produced the Balanced Budget Act of 1997. As Professor George C. Edwards III writes in our book of CSP case studies, ". . . both sides reached a historic agreement on achieving a balanced budget within five years. . . . Low-keyed good faith negotiations began shortly after the President submitted his budget, and senior White House officials held a series of private meetings with Members of Congress. Unlike the political posturing in late 1995 and early 1996, neither side focused on moving negotiations into the public arena. In the end, this made it easier for them to reach an agreement. . . . For Republicans, the budget agreement capped a balanced-budget, and tax-cutting drive. . . . For Clinton, the budget agreement represented perhaps his greatest legislative triumph." George Edwards, "The Balanced Budget Act of 1997," from *Triumphs and Tragedies of the Modern Presidency: Seventy-Six Case Studies in Presidential Leadership* (Washington, DC: Praeger Publishers, 2000), pp. 71–74.

cultivated the political center, joining with Republicans and fulfilling his promise to "end welfare as we know it," a monumental achievement that has reduced the states' welfare rolls, on average, 60 percent. Clinton coasted to easy reelection in 1996 over Senator Robert Dole and Ross Perot.

Then disaster: The President's sordid affair with a White House intern, Monica Lewinsky, and his attempt to cover it up, led to his House impeachment and the first Senate trial of a sitting President since Andrew Johnson. This episode showed that Clinton lacked Ronald Reagan's ability to get out of a hole. If Clinton had called in the longtime Washington attorney, Lloyd Cutler, and confessed privately of his shame, Cutler surely would have said, "Mr. President, brace yourself, make a complete public statement, get it all, I mean *all*, out." The result would have been public and political expressions of shame mixed with compassion and relief for perhaps several weeks, and then a President of enormous promise would have moved on. Instead, he lied before a grand jury in a civil case to cover up the affair, thus providing the legal grounds for impeachment.

But the Republican Congress was at fault as well. Unlike the bipartisan Congressional handling of the Nixon-era Watergate crisis, and the Reagan administration's Iran-Contra scandal, the extremely bitter and personal 1998-1999 Clinton warfare was reminiscent of the total ideological war between Andrew Johnson and the radical Republicans over Reconstruction. In the Senate trial, Senator Dianne Feinstein offered a constructive way out of the controversy, with a resolution stating that President Clinton "gave false and misleading testimony, and his actions have had the effect of impeding discovery of evidence of Judicial Proceedings." This resolution drew support from seventy-nine Senators from both parties, but was blocked by Republicans who wanted the criminal conviction that they clearly could not obtain. The loss of the vital, civil center left Congress dysfunctional, passive, and increasingly irrelevant.

Professor Fred Greenstein, in his book *The Presidential Difference: Leadership Style from FDR to Clinton*, labels his Clinton chapter, "The Undisciplined Bill Clinton." The same epithet can be applied to the Republicans and the undisciplined but often-brilliant Speaker of the House, Newt Gingrich. Clinton and Gingrich had in common something rare in most prominent politicians, a willingness to look over and across the horizon, tackle the big issues, and attempt to apply to them a new creativity. The tragedy is that there could have been a Clinton-Gingrich era of pragmatic cooperation, construction, and coming together on a range of long-term issues, as with their achievement on welfare reform.[*]

---

[*] Professor Robert Durant presents an informative analysis of Clinton's overall philosophical orientation, in which he shows that Clinton's "legislative, administrative and rhetorical record was informed throughout his political career by a core set of beliefs about the appropriate relationship between citizen and state and this is known as the New Covenant," using the biblical term. Along with the democratic leadership counsel, he aimed to change the perception of the Democratic Party from a "rights-based" to "responsibility based" policy agenda." Part of this strategy aimed to bring back the "Reagan Democrats." Clinton insisted that the New Covenant was not a "split-the-difference" approach; rather, the New Covenant was "beyond and not between, the ideologies of the left and right." One might argue that in the first two years of his Presidency, he lost his moorings, but with the 1994 election set back when he brought in Dick Morris, he returned to his New Covenant ideology, helped by the pull of the New Republican Congress. Then, with the Lewinsky affair and faced with impeachment, he shifted left to align himself with the Hill Democrats. Durant also notes that George W. Bush in 2000 adopted his own version of a "triangulation" strategy. Robert F. Durant, "A 'New' Covenant Kept: Core Values, Presidential Communications, and the Paradox of the Clinton Presidency," *Presidential Studies Quarterly* (September 2006, vol. 36:3), pp. 345–72.

On the post–Cold War foreign-policy front, credit goes to Bill Clinton for building America's positive image worldwide. He presided over a remarkable expansion of NATO to twenty-six members and the creation of a partners program to include for a total of forty-six other countries. During the Balkans conflict in the 1990s, he had success in Bosnia with the help of the skilled Richard Holbrooke and drew upon NATO to end the Serbian repression of ethnic Albanians in Kosovo. In all of this he had strong bipartisan support from Senators Bob Dole and John McCain, two war heroes who helped give him political clout.

At Camp David, in the waning months of his Presidency, he came close to a historic Israeli-Palestinian Agreement between Prime Minister Ehud Barak and Yasser Arafat, before the Palestinian leader inexplicably pulled out. It was a tough blow to an already embattled President, damaged by the Lewinsky affair, the deeply partisan atmosphere in Washington, and the looming end of his term.

George W. Bush: Courage Over Strategy

One must tread carefully when evaluating a sitting President, particularly in the case of George W. Bush, whose legacy will hinge on our success or failure in Iraq. The English historian C.V. Wedgewood wrote, "History is lived forward, but written backward."[47] Presidents often look different in retrospect than they did to observers at the time. Harry Truman and Ronald Reagan have both benefited dramatically from the passage of time and favorable reappraisals by historians. Warren Harding and Calvin Coolidge, on the other hand, enjoyed high ratings during their time but have since come to be seen as small, unremarkable men. At the same time, for us in 2008, judgment is inevitable, if we are to properly interpret the challenges and opportunities Bush will bequeath to his successor. Such an assessment will help the next President to avoid Bush's mistakes while building upon his successes.

In his 2000 party acceptance speech, George W. Bush pledged to be a "uniter," and not a "divider." For a time it looked as if his platform of "compassionate conservatism" might remake the political landscape by attracting liberals and conservatives alike to a set of policies that mixed conservative and progressive elements. A born-again Christian, Bush's upstanding private life offered a refreshing, attractive example for many Americans. Abroad, he promised he would pursue a modest foreign policy and eschew the interventions and "nation building" that defined Clinton's presidency. Finally, in his inaugural address, Bush issued a call for civility: "America, at its best, matches a commitment to principle with a concern for civility. . . . Civility is not a tactic or a sentiment. It is the determined choice of trust over cynicism, of community over chaos. And this commitment, if we keep it, is a way to shared accomplishment."[48]

Even though he lost the majority vote, he entered office and moved boldly, despite the lack of a strong mandate. His first accomplishment was a tax cut that Republicans cheered, but Democrats roundly criticized as favoring the rich. Regardless of that debate, the Bush years have seen recovery from a shallow recession suffered prior to the September 11, 2001 terrorist attacks. The discipline shown by the Federal Reserve brought low inflation and high job formation with increased productivity. President Bush moved toward the center and joined with Senator Ted Kennedy to craft the bipartisan education bill No Child Left Behind (NCLB), which is now up for reauthorization.

"Civility is not a tactic or a sentiment. It is the determined choice of trust over cynicism, of community over chaos. And this commitment, if we keep it, is a way to shared accomplishment."
—George W. Bush, First Inaugural Address

With the No Child Left Behind Act, Bush showed that a Republican could take education reform seriously and delivered impressive legislative results. The act set the extraordinary goal that all students would be proficient in mathematics and English by 2014, and it held schools accountable for the yearly improvement of all students. The bold legislation is not perfect, and Senator Kennedy later criticized the President for inadequate funding. Kennedy is certainly not alone, as most critics of NCLB argue that the Bush Administration has very significantly under funded NCLB at the state level and yet has required states to comply with all provisions of NCLB or risk losing federal funds.* Still, some supporters claim there are promising early results from this program, which broke with

---

*The criticisms of NCLB go well beyond inadequate funding. Another complaint is that NCLB encourages, and rewards, teaching children to score well on the test, rather than teaching with a primary goal of learning. As a result, teachers are pressured to teach a narrow set of test-taking skills and a test-limited range of knowledge. What's more, NCLB ignores many other vital subjects, including science, history, and foreign languages. In many cases, this has led to a drastic shortage of teachers. Critics have also argued that there should be some allowance for significant annual progress and growth—thus not tying all children to an identical goal. There are too many outside factors that cannot be controlled in the school setting. It would be hoped that a bipartisan consensus to maintain accountability would emerge, taking into account the lessons learned from the controversial initial run. The contribution made by the New Commission on the Skills of the American Workforce has called for the biggest changes in the American education system in a century. Commissioner Brock, echoes the urgency of these changes: "This proposal is radical? Yes. Hard to achieve? Of course. Essential? Absolutely. Our nation's schools are failing to educate our children, and that has to stop—else we condemn our own kids to ever lower incomes. We must act—now!" (www.skillscommission.org).

the traditional Republican aim to minimize government influence (particularly on education). "[T]here was a time," wrote *Washington Post* columnist Richard Cohen not long ago, "when no group of Republicans could convene without passing a resolution calling for the abolition of the Education Department and turning of the building—I am extrapolating here—into a museum of creationism." With NCLB, however, "Bush has extended the department's reach in a manner that Democrats could not envision."[49]

President Bush again showed his "compassionate conservatism" when he moved, for the second time, to nearly double the financing of the global fight against AIDS over the next five years. This doubling results in a $30 billion contribution to the President's AIDS initiative. Bush has advanced an increased awareness of this global issue throughout his terms and it has generated bipartisan support in Congress. Bush is rightfully proud that, in his words, "[Our] citizens are offering comfort to millions who suffer, and restoring the hope to those who feel forsaken."[50]

During the Bush Administration, the expansion of international trade promoted by Presidents George H. W. Bush and Bill Clinton has faced tough obstacles. Corporate outsourcing of U.S. jobs to China, India, and other emerging economies has generated widespread voter concern, especially among Democrats. This anxiety is easily understood. Every American benefits from lower prices of foreign-made goods and services, but the people who suffer are unemployed workers and their families and, sometimes, entire regions. Blame for this "unintended consequence" of job losses cannot be laid at either party's feet. Both Democratic and Republican Administrations and members of Congress have repeatedly supported global trade and foreign investment activities by U.S. corporations through such vehicles as fast-track trading, and bilateral and regional trade agreements. NAFTA and CAFTA are just two such examples.* But the mood has changed. Voters are voicing their concerns about job losses, and Democrats are questioning current government policies that favor unrestricted global investment and outsourcing. Economists, meanwhile, are trying to identify policies that would encourage more American companies retain their U.S. bases.** The evolution of both parties' positions on global trade will likely undergo significant developments in the years ahead.

Considering that both the President and the Vice President have served as executives of companies in the energy industry, it was significant that President Bush sponsored, and Congress passed, forward-looking energy legislation. On January 31, 2006, in his State of the Union address, President Bush joined a growing list of recent Presidents by stating that we must break our oil dependency. However, like his predecessors Gerald Ford and Jimmy Carter, Bush can be criticized for not yet giving enough teeth to his rhetoric. In his most promising remarks to date, Bush did assert at the G-8 summit in Heiligendamm, Germany, that he is now open to more aggressive measures to combat climate change, provided the fifteen nations most responsible for greenhouse gas emissions act in consent. Moreover, he has also advocated a "Twenty in Ten" plan that calls for cutting 20 per-

---

* In 2005, the Republican leadership and U.S. Trade Representative Robert Portman, a former Congressman, successfully reached out to Democrats to gain a narrow 217 to 215 passage of the CAFTA.

** Former Treasury Secretary Robert Rubin, who provided distinguished leadership during the Clinton Administration, helped found the Hamilton Project at the Brookings Institution to provide "fresh ideas on the drivers shaping the global economy, the road out of poverty and the rise of new economic powers." Ralph Gomory, former President of the Alfred P. Sloan Foundation, has written about the danger of outsourcing critical U.S. industries and the need to retain U.S. corporations that produce "high value-added" jobs.

cent of our gasoline consumption in ten years. Still, the administration is not moving aggressively enough against a problem that may well define the coming decades.

In setting the policy and tone of this Presidency, former Defense Secretary Dick Cheney wields far more influence than any previous Vice President. He has made it clear that his advice to the President has been to promote Executive authority: "In thirty-four years, I have repeatedly seen an erosion of the powers and the ability of the president of the United States to do his job . . . I do think that to some extent now, we've been able to restore the legitimate authority of the presidency."[51] As the historian James MacGregor Burns has noted, "Cheney saw Bush every morning and several times each day. If Bush believed his father had failed because he was wishy-washy, Cheney's advice for a successful Presidency—stay on the offensive and push back hard against critics; be assertive and decisive and never waver—strengthened [Bush's] instincts."[52]

Aiming to play a central role in decisions related to security and foreign policy, the Vice President in effect built his own national security staff. He was able, at least in one dramatic case, to secretly bypass the official national security process. On November 13, 2001, CNN revealed that the Vice President had the President sign an order stipulating that foreign terror suspects held by the United States were to be stripped of access to civilian or military courts, domestic or foreign. The *Washington Post* has reported that this broadcast was the first time Secretary of State Colin Powell and National Security Advisor Condoleezza Rice had heard about their Administration's stance on detainees.[53]

The wisdom or necessity of Cheney's recommendations notwithstanding, such happenings added to the erosion of the Administration's trust, and violated the letter and spirit of the National Security Act of 1947, which requires the involvement of the Secretary of State and the National Security Advisor in the security decision-making process. As we shall see in Part II, this rupture was largely responsible for a flawed and insufficient plan for going to war against Iraq.

Before these inside dealings, President Bush enjoyed immense popularity with his inclusive leadership during the three months following the September 11 attacks. The Bush Doctrine, set forth in the *National Security Strategy* report of 2002, offered an innovative and prescient framework for dealing with the unprecedented threat of global terror. He believes that, in an age of elusive and fast-moving enemies, the United States will occasionally have to take drastic measures, like preemptive attacks on states harboring terrorists, to protect the nation from harm.

As Cold War historian John Lewis Gaddis has pointed out, "The Bush Doctrine does not reject deterrence and containment." It simply—and justly—insists "upon the need to supplement these familiar strategies" with preemption.[54] When Bush lost his post-9/11 momentum in the wake of an undermanned and underplanned invasion of Iraq, it was not the fault of the Bush Doctrine. It was the fault of misguided implementation based on an ideological mind-set that held that reconstruction would take care of itself.

Following 9/11, the Use of Force Act gave the President authority, with only one dissenting vote in Congress, to use "all necessary and appropriate force against those nations, organizations, or persons he determines planned, authorized, committed, or aided"[55] the September 11 attacks. Bush followed up his speaking to the public by going to Congress for specific statutory action for 2001 to commit U.S. troops to combat in Afghanistan and subsequently in 2002 to undertake military action against Iraq. As Louis Fisher notes, "It would be wrong to say that Congress decided on war. It decided only that President Bush should decide." Fisher goes on to note that in this respect, the resolution mirrored the 1964 Gulf of Tonkin resolution: ". . . the reservations are virtually identical in transferring to the President the sole decision to go to war and determine its scope and duration."[56] With both resolutions Congress invested profound power in the Executive branch—a move that many Democrats and some Republicans have come to regret.

For the Bush Administration, there has been no decisive transformation—no moment comparable to 1939, when Franklin Roosevelt declared his intention to change course from Dr. New Deal to Dr. Win the War. One reason for this has undoubtedly been the influence of Karl Rove, whose sway over White House policy exceeds that of any political advisor in recent history.

> ∾ **For the Bush Administration, there has been no decisive transformation— no moment comparable to 1939, when FDR declared his intention to change course from Dr. New Deal to Dr. Win the War.**

"The architect" of victories in 2000 and 2004, Rove is a close student of political history, but his favorite studies miss critical lessons. He tried to model Bush's strategies on the sweeping McKinley victories of 1896, when, with his campaign manager Mark Hanna, he engineered a political realignment that set the stage for a decades-long Republican ascendancy. But Rove—and, for that matter, others in the White House— do not seem to have spent time studying our greatest war Presidents, particularly Abraham Lincoln, Franklin Roosevelt, Harry Truman, and Dwight Eisenhower. If Rove—like FDR's Harry Hopkins—had urged the President to abandon an overtly partisan strategy for one more suited to war-time unity and mobilization, history may have been different. Colin Powell, the Cabinet member who might have helped to bring about this tipping point, was marginalized not long after 9/11.

In 2007, George C. Edwards III and Desmond S. King led a group of fifteen political scientists in conducting a broad study of the Bush Presidency. The resulting publication, entitled *The Polarized Presidency of George W. Bush*, reaches somber conclusions. According to Edwards and King, Bush is "the most polarizing President in polling history" and has been since his inauguration. Moreover, as of May 2004 "the difference between his approval among Republicans (89 percent) and Democrats (12 percent), was an astounding 77 percentage points . . . no President, dating back to Harry Truman, has had a partisan gap above 70 points in any Gallup poll in a reelection year."[57] While the President had strong majority support for his initial decision to go to war, by 2005 "this division was much greater than it had been for any other U.S. military engagement since the Second World War, including the Vietnam War."[58] This phenomenon arises partly from the tenacity with which Bush has supported his own policies, as well as his unwavering campaign to promote a Republican majority, often conducted with considerable political skill.

If the nation were not at war (the President's own term), and if we did not face so many simultaneous near- and long-term challenges at home and abroad, Bush's time in office could provide an interesting and in many ways remarkable Presidential case study for historians and political scientists. His success in two elections might be the envy of Democrats. Considering the challenges to the Presidency laid out in this document, however, as well as the argument that the nation can only surmount these hurdles by coming together across party lines, the polarization phenomenon seems threatening and carries implications for the success of the next Presidency. This tendency toward divisiveness was exacerbated during the Clinton Administration and has been brewing for a long while in Congress due to the consequences of redistricting. There remains, as well, the hovering specter of the Vietnam disaster and the long aftermath of the 1960s.

Mired in Iraq and battles over executive privilege related to his Attorney General, Bush has turned to policy matters closer to home. His immigration reform initiatives are marked by that same courage and stubbornness reflected in the President's actions concerning the war in Iraq. But there are also signs of the bipartisan innovator who campaigned as a "uniter" in 2000. The *New York Times's* Jim Rutenberg and Carl Hulse point out that "President Bush's advocacy of an immigration overhaul and his attack on critics of the plan [have provoked] an unusually intense backlash from conservatives,"[59] while simultaneously winning support from prominent Democrats like Senator Ted Kennedy. But again we see the fallout from eroded credibility in other arenas: Bush lacked the political capital to push an immigration agreement through Congress, as prominent Republican Senators, including the Minority Leader, abandoned him in the Senate. With no plan for dealing with twelve million illegal immigrants in the country, the next President will inherit this divisive issue at a time when the need for unity has rarely been greater.*

---

* In an analysis under the label, "Charting a New Imperial Presidency," Andrew Rudalevige describes the regaining of Executive power after the Watergate and Vietnam setbacks culminating with the George W. Bush Administration assertion of unitary power. One example of this occurred in 2005 when Congress overwhelmingly approved a blanket ban on torture. Bush in his signing statement said he would implement the revision in a manner consistent with the Constitutional authority of the President to oversee the unitary Executive branch and as Commander-in-Chief. Of course there has been a long history of interpretive exceptions in Presidential signing statements, but this torturing restriction passed by a Republican Congress on a matter of national and international focus raises the Presidential action to a new level. Rudalevige argues that "we want

There is one spot of good amidst all the bad news: some polling shows that when confronted with important issues, the people go beyond special interests and pulls together to confront obstacles. This Center has put together a list of over 200 leaders, including former heads of the Democratic and Republican National Committees, diverse religious leaders, university heads, CEOs of businesses, and a range of former members of Congress who have all signed a document calling for civility and inclusive leadership in facing our national challenges.[60] Furthermore, three remarkable bipartisan events, without parallel since World War II, have occurred, in which leading Republicans and Democrats worked together on two commissions and one study group to discuss controversial intelligence matters and the best course for the Iraq War.

Collaboration amid Polarization:
Three Bipartisan Commissions

During George W. Bush's administration, three bipartisan initiatives have emerged from outstanding leaders in Congress: the 9/11 Commission, the Commission on the Intelligence Capabilities of the United States Regarding Weapons of Mass Destruction, and the Baker-Hamilton Iraq Study Group (ISG). These are examples of the democratic system of gov-

---

men and women of ambition and abilities to serve as our Presidents. But, to pledge that their preferences should without need of persuasion become policy, that they should as a matter of course substitute command for coalition building," is to cede something of the soul of self-governance. The dangers of unilateral authority are immense, because once these claims are asserted, they logically admit to no limits. Andrew Rudalevige, "The Decline and Resurgence and Decline (and Resurgence?) of the Congress: Charting a New Imperial Presidency," *Presidential Studies Quarterly* (September 2006).

ernment at its best: diverse minds and respected figures were brought together to address shared problems, putting aside their party agendas for the sake of a common struggle. The American public, after all, expects nothing less.

The first and by far the most encompassing of these initiatives was the 9/11 Commission. This commission came about largely through the work of the families of the victims of the terrorist attacks, who wanted to know why the nation had been left so defenseless. Over the Administration's initial objections, Congress established the Commission with former Governor Thomas Kean as Chairman and former Congressman Lee Hamilton as Vice Chairman. They made three wise decisions. The first was to have this bipartisan commission staffed by nonpartisan personnel. The second was to hold hearings publicly, so as to keep officials accountable and to communicate the Commission's work directly to the American people. Kean and Hamilton also decided that the report would be available to the public at a low cost in bookstores. Among its many recommendations, the Commission called for the establishment of a Director of National Intelligence to coordinate the government's many varied intelligence agencies, as well as a comprehensive restructure of Congress to protect the homeland from future threats.

After publicizing its report in July 2004, the two chairs established a separate 501c(3), the 9/11 Public Discourse Project, "aimed at fulfilling the 9/11 Commission's original mandate of guarding against future terrorist attacks, while adhering strictly to the same bipartisan and independent principles that have guided it over the last twenty months."[61] Kean stated that the Commission had been born from "unity of purpose" and that its greatest virtue was bipartisan credibility in the push to enact its recommendations.[62]

The Commission on the Intelligence Capabilities of the United States Regarding Weapons of Mass Destruction, co-chaired by former Senator Chuck Robb and Judge Laurence Silberman, is also worthy of the next President's study. This commission was set up to assess whether the U.S. intelligence community "was sufficiently authorized, organized, equipped, trained, and resourced" to identify and warn of a terrorist attack with weapons of mass

> ∽ **"Trust is the coin of the realm," is a mantra the next President would do well to revive.**

destruction (WMD) on American soil. The Commission concluded that the U.S. intelligence community had been "dead wrong" in its prewar assessments and judgments of Iraq's WMD capacity. This misjudgment was due to the "fragmented, loosely managed, and poorly coordinated"[63] relations between intelligence agencies, as well as failure to communicate among the intelligence agencies, Congress, and the Executive branch. Subsequently, President Bush accepted sixty-nine of the Commission's seventy-three recommendations.

The Baker-Hamilton ISG represented the last of three bipartisan initiatives. This extraordinary net assessment involved over 250 experts and officials. Despite party differences, the 10 principals worked to produce a comprehensive review of what it called the "grave and deteriorating" situation in Iraq. Its report detailed seventy-nine recommendations, which addressed every angle of the situation from internal security and economics to international relations. Thanks to widespread consultations on Capital Hill in the autumn, the strategic framework Baker-Hamilton laid out enjoyed strong bipartisan support. For the first time in months, there was a proposal for a comprehensive and widely endorsed way forward. As Congressman Frank Wolf, who first conceived of the idea of the ISG, requested of cochairs James Baker and Lee Hamilton when they met to select members: "I want a diverse group of Americans who love their country more than their party."[64] This remarkable near consensus on Capitol Hill fell apart, however, in the wake of the President's decision to launch a five combat brigade "surge." The lack of in-depth consultations on Capitol Hill pertaining to the "surge" initiative stands in shocking contrast to the extensive Baker-Hamilton consultations.

Washington may seem paralyzed with partisanship, but these three commissions show the next President we still possess the will to come together to address tough problems.* Furthermore, learning the art of utilizing wisely constructed bipartisan commissions to deal with daunting challenges can serve the next President greatly.[65] The approach began with the collaborations of Harry S. Truman and Herbert Hoover.

---

*Although these three commissions deserve considerable praise, their limitations should be noted if only to provide an equitable perspective. For the 9/11 Commission and the Commission on the Intelligence Capabilities of the United States Regarding Weapons of Mass Destruction, the weaknesses lie in conditions which limited the research and examination processes. The commissions accepted Presidential Administration cooperation that focused on the intelligence processes which, however, failed to study the policy implementation of that intelligence. The third panel, the ISG, was based upon an agreement with the Executive branch that the ISG would be "forward looking" and therefore there was no examination of past decision-making processes with regard to the Iraq conflict. As we can recall from our assessment of Pearl Harbor, the failure involved neglecting to distinguish "noise" from the alarming signals, but more importantly failing to provide the analysis and interpretation of those signals for the decision-making process. In the 9/11 and WMD Commissions, the misuse of intelligence and "mind-sets" that blocked dissent occurred just as it had in Pearl Harbor. The only commission since World War II that examined the entire decision-making process was the Murphy Commission. President Gerald Ford filled a vacancy with Vice President Nelson Rockefeller, Mike Mansfield, when two other commissioners split from the final report.

CHAPTER 4

LESSONS FOR THE NEXT PRESIDENT

W HAT EMERGES from this quick look at some of the peaks and valleys of the American Presidency are several clear and crucial lessons.

Dynamic Strategy

First, the next President must have a dynamic strategy to unite the nation in the face of severe challenges at home and abroad. America has come together to confront similar dangers before—during the Revolution, the Constitutional Convention, and the World Wars—and must do so again. Bipartisan coalitions in Congress, as well as the commissions like those outlined previously, can be effective tools. Justice Robert H. Jackson, in a 1952 Supreme Court opinion, stated that we must never forget that "Presidential powers are not fixed, but fluctuate depending upon their disjunction or conjunction with those of Congress."[1] This observation remains true today. When a President acts in accordance with the will of the Congress, presidential authority is at its maximum because it is buttressed by the prerogatives of both bodies. When measures are incompatible with the wishes of the Congress, however, the President's authority shrinks to "its lowest ebb." The preeminent constitutional scholar Edward Corwin noted, "The Constitution . . . is an invitation to struggle for the privilege of directing American foreign policy."[2] A wise new President knows that Article II of the Constitution gives the Executive branch the advantage and enables them to build effective coalitions through listening and persuasion.

∽ **Trust has two components: truthfulness— being honest and straight forward— and accountability.**

Trust

A prerequisite of uniting the nation—and the second lesson of this profile of our next President—is the importance of winning the trust of Congress and the Nation. "Trust is the coin of the realm" was the mantra in the Eisenhower White House, and the next President would do well to revive it.[*] Trust has two components: truthfulness—being honest and straight forward—and accountability. At times the nation has trusted a President as an honest individual, but not a competent one. Such was the case for James Madison during the poorly-executed War of 1812 and George W. Bush in the Iraq War. Ulysses S. Grant was an honest man, but incompetent when it came to managing his corrupt associates. Prior to Pearl Harbor, Franklin Roosevelt ran a tremendous risk in his covert actions to save the British, but subsequently held the trust of the nation as a war leader.

War leadership cannot be sustained over a period of time without public trust. On the other hand, tremendously able men have often failed to inspire the nation's trust. The collapse of trust in Richard Nixon is the most egregious exam-

---

[*] This expression comes from Bryce Harlow, who was President Eisenhower's liaison to Capitol Hill. Harlow knew that trust in Ike was his greatest asset.

ple. As Theodore Roosevelt noted, the President is the trustee of the nation, and a good trustee must be able to perform with competency as the return on the investment of trust.

Leadership

The third lesson is for the next President to lead his party, not just follow it. This can be done by establishing behind-the-scenes rapport with both Republicans and Democrats on Capitol Hill. Thomas Jefferson was the first President who was also a true leader of his party, the Democrat-Republicans. Modern Presidents are weakened if they lose the support of their parties. However, Presidents with the greatest leadership skills have been able to lead the party—rather than let the party lead them. This is a difficult balance to maintain, and some George W. Bush advisors would argue that his father lost his reelection bid because the party abandoned him. James Madison led his party in an entirely different direction following the War of 1812 debacle, along with his successor James Monroe, transformed his party and Presidency. Dwight Eisenhower was often accused of being apolitical, but he shifted his party from isolationism to internationalism. Ronald Reagan took his party with him, but shrewdly avoided divisive social issues. Today, George W. Bush's failure to develop strong relations with Capitol Hill has deprived him of transformational capability.

Courage

The fourth lesson is the importance of courage. It took courage for Andrew Jackson to stand up to John Calhoun during the nullification controversy; for Abraham Lincoln to go against his Cabinet and reinforce Fort Sumter; and for Harry Truman to fire the legendary General Douglas MacArthur. At the same time, it is well to remember Aristotle's insight that courage is

the mean between rashness and timidity. Overweening bold-
ness is a vice that leads to stubbornness and isolation, as we
saw in Woodrow Wilson's failure to pass the Treaty of Ver-
sailles through Congress and George W. Bush's attack on
Baghdad without a plan for the peace.

When smart Presidents have fallen into holes—John
Kennedy after the Bay of Pigs invasion and Ronald Reagan
during Iran-Contra—they have had the courage and intelli-
gence to admit their mistakes and learn from them. But these
are "short-term" crises. Addressing "long-term" crises such as
deficits, Social Security, and Medicare will take the courage of
a Franklin Roosevelt or a Lincoln.

Curbing Arrogance

The fifth lesson is to be on guard against hubris. Richard
Nixon famously kept an "enemies list." His name should have
been on the top. As Pogo said, "We have met the enemy . . .
and he is us." The same is true for many Presidents, but not all.
Reagan had a self-deprecating humor and easy self-confidence;
his ego, unlike Nixon, didn't need protective armor. George
Washington, humble in a more classical manner, resigned his
command of the Continental Army after the Revolution and
refused to serve a third term as President. Hence, he became
the model "servant leader."

The President-elect in 2008 should recall the requirement
that the Roman Republic laid on any conquering general
returning to Rome. During the celebratory parade through the
city, a slave rode next to him in his chariot, whispering:
"Remember, you too are mortal." When the new Administra-
tion piles in to the White House in January 2009 they will find
themselves tempted to forget this. This warning against hubris
also applies to the new Presidential staff, especially in terms of
their Congressional relations.

A Talented Team

The sixth lesson is to organize the Executive Branch and build a cabinet of talented advisors and department leaders who will be frank, focused, and coordinated, outreaching to the best of the public sector. Trust and courage are simply not enough; effective and innovative organization is needed. The new President must define a proper role for the Vice President, as coordinator and unifier. This includes building synergies and coordination within the Executive Branch and partnerships with the Congress.

The Vice President should ensure an effective management structure to assist the President and department heads in their efforts to translate abstract policy into practical results. The process laid out in the National Security Act *still* offers one of the best guides for bringing integrity to Executive decision-making. George Washington's first term, Franklin Roosevelt during the Second World War, and Harry Truman's term are case studies in effective Cabinet-building. Like FDR, a wise President will keep a "George Marshall" around to tell him privately when he is "dead wrong."

Grand Strategy

The seventh lesson involves the importance of communicating a transformational vision backed up with a truly comprehensive "grand" strategy for the years ahead. The new President will face compounding national challenges, and he or she must rise to the occasion. As Part II will further explain, Abraham Lincoln was a masterful grand strategist during the Civil War, as was Franklin Roosevelt during the Second World War. Dwight Eisenhower's planning laid the framework for American policy in the Cold War. Often there is no better way to forge a larger vision than to use commissions and special panels that tap the creative policy centers and best minds throughout the country—and across party lines—to devise innovative, practical measures. The commissions we have focused on in this section as well as the Greenspan Social Security Commission and the earlier Hoover Commissions show how to obtain results.

The Challenge

Of all the lessons, creating a dynamic vision, both realistic and achievable, may be the most challenging. Recent years have seen an erosion of the nation's strategic aptitude, with worrying results. The noble visions of Woodrow Wilson and George W. Bush reveal the dangers of vision without pathways to achieve results. The art of strategy is the art of developing pathways, not just setting grand goals. In the following section, we will explore in detail the idea of "grand strategy" and lay out what the next President needs to do to formulate an effective one in our global age.

If the walls of the White House could talk, these are some of the lessons that we believe would be heard. It is a wonder that, for well over two centuries, Presidents have not drawn nearly enough on the accumulated experience of their predecessor's successes, mistakes, and failures.

2009 is the year to change that.

PART II

"So first of all let me assert
my firm belief that the only
thing we have to fear . . .
is fear itself . . . nameless,
unreasoning, unjustified
terror which paralyzes
needed efforts to convert
retreat into advance."

FRANKLIN DELANO ROOSEVELT,
Inaugural Speech. March 4, 1933

CHAPTER 5

SIX ELEMENTS OF A NATIONAL STRATEGY

T HE END OF the Cold War left the United States as the world's only superpower and rendered its policies of containment and deterrence—the concerted effort to limit Soviet influence while avoiding nuclear war—obsolete. We have existed in a post-Soviet world for seventeen years, but despite the tragic wake-up call on September 11, 2001, and protracted wars in Iraq and Afghanistan, we have not yet fully adapted to its realities.

In addition to the traits of leadership enumerated in the first part of this book, the next President will need a grand strategy to unite and mobilize the nation in a new age of multidimensional challenges.

The Evolving Nature of the Threat

Since the end of the Second World War, the world has been arranged in a set of three overlapping paradigms. During the Cold War, the United States had a central adversary—the Soviet Union—whose mission was to expand territorially while protecting the Communist system. Since the Soviets believed in the "historic inevitability" of their dominance, the doctrine of MAD—Mutually Assured Destruction—offered a baseline of national security—a line which no rational Soviet would dare cross. Broadly speaking, the world was divided into two spheres, in which allegiances were formal and predictable. Following the end of the Cold War, the order of rigid alliances gave way to the second paradigm, in which decentralized threats defined a complex and constantly shifting world order. This period saw the rise in localized conflicts—the Balkans war, Somalia, and the first Gulf War. They were contained, but messy. Out of this flux came violence perpetrated in the name of radical Islam, a third paradigm.

Today, we face threats from rogue powers, non-state terrorist groups and a hybrid of both, united by extremist ideology, tyrannical leaders, or religiously inspired antagonism. This third paradigm does not follow the Cold War logic of deterrence. The nature of the conflict does not conform to the zero-sum game realist model of the first paradigm, and instead requires an understanding of different priorities than those determined by a bipolar balance of power. The United States has largely failed to understand the deep-set cultural and religious beliefs that suicide terrorists use to justify their actions, including their nuclear aspirations. This new playing field throws the strategic equation upside down, and introduces new uncertainties. With deterrence no longer a viable primary strategy, the United States and its allies must complicate or frustrate the new multidimensional threats by building obstacles to success, destroying financial support, undermining recruitment, and building coalitions against terrorism.[*]

---

[*] A previous writing of mine focuses on this subject, "U.S. Global Policy: Toward an Agile Strategy," has been briefed to the Army, Navy, and Air Force war colleges and it is interesting that in the playback from the students, the university noted that just as important as agile forces, was the need for agile minds. David M. Abshire, "U.S. Global Policy: Toward an Agile Strategy," *The Washington Quarterly* (Washington, DC: Spring 1996) 19:2, pp. 41–61.

Without the due-diligence it takes to truly understand the nature of threats, it is only a matter of time before another attack will slip through the security cracks. The most dangerous threat for a strategist, and our next President, is to fall prey to a misguided mind-set as a result of a breakdown in the Executive decision-making process. The next President must fully employ and utilize the President's Foreign Intelligence Advisory Board (PFIAB) in conjunction with a new contingency capability for National Security Council Staff. This would serve as an insurance policy against foreign policy and security failures.

> ∾ The United States has largely failed to understand the deep-set cultural and religious beliefs that suicide terrorists use to justify their actions, including their nuclear aspirations.

While tactics and threats change, strategies focused on encouraging and fostering unity of effort and freedom of action remain high priorities. In this strange new geopolitical landscape, characterized by multidimensional threats, unpredictable and complicated alliances, new financial powers, and the rise of non-state terrorist actors (often with rogue-state backing), process and strategy are more important than ever.

During the Cold War, Washington strategists exhibited, to borrow terminology popularized by the philosopher Isaiah Berlin, the "mind of the hedgehog."[1] They concentrated on defeating a fixed, unitary opponent. Today we don't have this kind of clarity. Indeed the greatest danger is inflexibility, the consequence of fixed mind-sets, which too frequently in recent years have preempted effective strategy. We need to cultivate the agile "mind of the fox."

Indeed, successful strategy has always been agile. We now need to deal with a diversity of smaller, asymmetrical challenges: the overwhelming threat of terrorism, particularly nuclear, biological, and cyberterrorism; the growing need for energy independence and sustainability; the rise of potential political and economic rivals such as China and India; the Middle East in turmoil, as well as a host of regional ethnic conflicts and failed states. To do this we need a grand strategy that fuses fiscal, political, technological, cultural, and psychological elements. In the chapters to come we offer our thoughts as to how one could craft and implement such a strategy. It is important to realize that a focus on agility in strategy should not be confused with our national goals, which remain constant objectives to achieve.

A Primer on Strategy

But first of all, what is strategy? Many people think that a strategy is synonymous with a plan, but this is misleading. Indeed, it is the opposite of a static blueprint, for it must be able to constantly adapt to changing circumstances. By the same token, strategy is not a science, because human affairs do not occur with the same certainty that natural and physical sciences do. Strategy-making is the process of developing, revising, and adapting pathways to achieve our goals while making sure a reasoned relationship exists between means and ends. In order to be strategic, one must not only be a keen intellect, but also a wise judge of human nature, particularly in competitive situations. I have always been partial to the classical military view, which considers strategy an art. The greatest practitioners of this art—Alexander the Great, Napoleon Bonaparte, Robert E. Lee, and Douglas MacArthur to name a few—have won famous victories over superior forces by going for vulnerability with surprise and "upsetting the enemy's center of gravity."* Disrupting that center has become

> ∞ **The next President will need a grand strategy to unite and mobilize the nation in a new age of multidimensional challenges.**

all the more difficult in the fight against terrorism organized in the name of God. However this fight becomes all the more important because this terrorism increasingly decentralized and self-generating nature uses religion as a motivating factor.

Today, much of the cutting edge "strategic thinking" takes place in the highly competitive business world, where both the players and the ultimate objective (the bottom line) are fairly clearly defined. But many of the key elements of strategy apply just as well to government, politics, and the military as they do to business. Almost twenty-five years ago, Harvard Business School's Michael Porter wrote his influential book *Competitive Strategies* as a text for the business world, but it was adopted in the Pentagon and War College.[2] Porter sought to show how leaders could maximize their competitive advantage over opponents by reading "market signals" and breaking down internal compartments to achieve more effective overall functioning. He showed how strategy requires a combination of rigorous analysis and intuitive sensitivity to the dynamic forces, which shape different, shifting circumstances.

In recent years, a number of scholars and statesmen have tried their hands at crafting a grand plan for the post-9/11 world. Each, in their own way, seeks the mantle of George Kennan, author of the last truly comprehensive American strategy, Cold War containment doctrine.[3] While it is fair to say that none of these contemporary figures have yet to enjoy

---

*This phrase was used by Gulf War General Norman Schwarzkopf and Colin Powell. The examples of strategic brilliance are many. To name a few: Alexander the Great's smashing victory of the Persian King Darius; Hannibal's victory over the Romans at Cannae; Napoleon similarly defeating the Russo-Austrian Army in 1806 at Austerlitz; Lee and Jackson outnumbered two to one, outflanking General Hooker at Chancellorsville; or MacArthur's 1950 landing at Incheon which turned the flank of the North Korean army. Such strategy is an art still studied at our military academies and war colleges.

Kennan's stature and influence, there have been many important contributions. Of particular note, Professor Francis Fukuyama's *America at the Crossroads* lays out a policy of "realistic Wilsonianism," which emphasizes the need for America to use many and overlapping international institutions, when possible, to gain international legitimacy and enhanced strength.[4] Dennis Ross's book has more recently drawn attention to the neglected art of "statecraft," the skillful use of economic, diplomatic, and military tools and handmaiden of strategic vision.[5] Meanwhile Professor Anne-Marie Slaughter has thoughtfully reappraised the values that should underlie our foreign policy in *The Idea That Is America*,[6] while former national security adviser, Zbigniew Brzezinski's *Second Chance* assesses the performances of our three post-Cold War Presidents in international affairs.[7] Fred Iklé has stretched our thinking beyond the present planning for the war on terror in his book *Annihilation from Within*, where a characteristic upstart will be able to threaten or attack a nation from within with nuclear capabilities. These and other books contribute much, but there has, to date, been rather little attention paid to the essential components of strategy and how these components may be applied successfully today.[*]

---

[*] An exception to this is the incisive article by Charles A. Kupchan and Peter L. Trubowitz, "Grand Strategy for a Divided America," *Foreign Affairs* (July/August 2007). The Kennan influence in crafting the doctrine on containment might be compared to that of Naval War College president, Alfred Thayer Mahan's doctrine of sea power. He called for large merchant marine battle ships, protected commercial routes, and a canal through the isthmus of Panama, along with bases in the Caribbean and Pacific. His acolytes were Theodore Roosevelt, Senator Henry Cabot Lodge, Elihu Root, John Hayes, and Admiral George Dewey. Mahan influenced our move into the Pacific following the Spanish American War and was considerably responsible for the robust Navy at the time of the First World War. For

Strategy is a multidimensional art. Its practitioners need to take into account numerous factors: the balance of long-term goals with short-term realities, the mainte-nance of public understanding and trust, the management and promo-

> ∽ **The next President must relearn the art of strategy.**

tion of technological progress, and the organization of deci-sion-making and seeking competitive advantage. Beyond these shifting, elusive concerns, strategy must focus on two basic requirements: maintaining unity of effort and enhancing free-dom of action. Our opponents, beginning with al-Qaeda, aim to destroy this essential armor. They rely on our mismanage-ment to assist in the deterioration of our country's security and the core principles on which it was founded.

With a national debt of $4.8 trillion dollars—an increasing portion of which is in foreign hands—and mounting health care, education, and Social Security crises, the nation's financial free-dom of action has rarely been so constrained. With our ongoing commitments in Iraq, our military is stretched to untenable lev-els and we are tactically exposed around the world. Our adver-saries know this. Our diplomatic leverage—our powers of persuasion—have become limited. Old friends in and beyond Europe are suspicious of American power and motives. Mean-while, the nuclear threat of missiles and smuggled devices into the nation is on the rise.

Working within Washington for fifty years, I, for one, have never seen a more seriously alarming situation. These com-pounding circumstances declare, loud and clear, that the next President must relearn the art of strategy.

---

more on the Kennan-Mahan comparison see Warren Zimmermann's book *The First Great Triumph* (New York, Farrar, Straus and Giroux, 2002), pp. 85–122.

Abraham Lincoln studied strategy. In the darkest days of the Civil War, he visited the Library of Congress and took out classics of military strategy by Carl von Clausewitz and Napoleon Bonaparte.

Clausewitz observed that one should never go to war for its own sake, but rather to advance some political end. Political objectives must govern strategic ones. Applied to Iraq, we grasp this concept correctly when it is said there cannot be a "military solution" in Baghdad. Indeed, military force is but one form of power, and sometimes the least effective form.

"The moral is to the physical as three is to one," Napoleon once remarked.[8] For him, the human factors—perceptions, beliefs, morale—were three times as important as the size of his armies. Today it remains true that economic incentives, as well as financial, diplomatic, and cultural forces—the tools Joseph Nye has called "soft power"—are often more effective than physical force.[9] All of these combine to create the concept of grand strategy.* "The perfect battle," Sun Tzu observed in the sixth century, "is the one you don't have to fight."[10] NATO offers the most compelling recent example: in the Cold War under America's low-key leadership, the Alliance defeated the Warsaw Pact without ever firing a shot.

If strategy is the art of winning wars, tactics make up the art of waging battles fought for a reasoned, strategic purpose. In military history, however, time and again, a focus on battles has become a substitute for good strategy. Such happened in the attrition warfare of 1915 and 1916 in World War I, and in

---

* Joseph Nye and former Deputy Secretary of State Richard Armitage recently partnered to head the Commission on Smart Power, based at the Center for Strategic and International Studies in Washington, DC. A "smart" power strategy unites "hard" (military) and "soft" to restore America's standing in the world and address current and future challenges.

the McNamara-Westmoreland phase of the Vietnam War. In Iraq in 2007, we have debated the advantages and disadvantages of the "surge," but have not always properly appreciated that the temporary increase of troops was a tactic of limited duration. Unfortunately, however, the "surge" was perceived as a strategy. There can be no victory without political progress: a stable, representative government in Iraq and a sufficient bipartisan consensus in Washington to support the process.

Technology can be of crucial importance, affecting both strategy and tactics. In five years—a longer period than it took American scientists at Los Alamos to create the Atomic Bomb—we have yet to produce an effective deterrent to the Improvised Explosive Devices that are the terrorists' most effective military weapon in Iraq.

Still, technology can also be a false god. We entered the war believing that technological superiority would give us unchallenged "information supremacy:" we would anticipate and defuse our enemies' movements with superior intelligence, lightning quick communication, and precise weaponry. Such happened in the conventional phase of the Iraqi War. In the second phase, our enemies now seem better able to anticipate our actions, while Americans struggle with the intricacies of Iraqi and Afghan tribal politics and the near impossibility of spotting terrorists embedded in the civilian population.

But even with a sound strategy and the strongest tactical advantages, the next President will have to fight real battles as well as Sun Tzu's "perfect" ones. The country's forty-fourth President will almost certainly take office at a time of war, with the military heavily deployed in Iraq and Afghanistan and the abiding threat of a terrorist attack on our homeland. To become an effective grand strategist in this context, the new President should study our two greatest wartime Presidents, Abraham Lincoln and Franklin Roosevelt, whose conduct exhibited six crucial characteristics.

Lincoln and Roosevelt were able to respond decisively to crises; set priorities; mobilize the nation; maintain unity; develop a trenchant public strategy; and offer a vision of the country's future beyond the conflict at hand.

In the upcoming chapter, we will compare different Presidential strategies, with a special focus on Lincoln and Roosevelt, and analyze the relation of both to the current situation under outgoing President George W. Bush. Any analysis is limited as this stage, but essential, for the next President will take over where Bush leaves off. As noted in Part I, we recognize the limitations of making definitive judgments before a completed Presidential term in a part of history. Finally we will suggest what the next President needs to do in each of the six areas above to restore American strength at home and stature abroad in the post-Cold War era.

CHAPTER 6

RESPONDING DECISIVELY TO A CRISIS

L EADERS ARE often made or unmade by their first exposure to crisis. No sooner had Abraham Lincoln been inaugurated than the Confederates demanded the evacuation of Fort Sumter in South Carolina's Charleston Harbor. In the face of staunch opposition from the Army's commanding general, Winfield Scott, a hero of the Mexican War; Secretary of State William Seward and others in his Cabinet, the inexperienced Lincoln, made the decision to hold and resupply Fort Sumter. When the Confederate Army forced its surrender, Lincoln immediately called for the enlistment of 75,000 militiamen for ninety days. It was his strategic judgment that decisively galvanized and mobilized the North.

Franklin Roosevelt initially made a terrible tactical mistake in overruling Admiral James Richardson and leaving the Pacific fleet exposed at Pearl Harbor in Hawaii, calculating that the fleet would deter a Japanese attack rather than serve as a target for one (fortunately, our carriers were at sea on December 7, 1941).* But soon after the attack Roosevelt

---

* Roosevelt and his staff simply misjudged Japanese intentions. He thought that a Japanese attack on U.S. possessions was illogical and felt that Japan would only strike British and Dutch territory in Southeast Asia, which would avoid bringing America into the war. In the introduction to Roberta Wohlstetter's classic, *Pearl Harbor:*

righted himself. Even with the loss of eight battleships, he rallied, calling December 7th a "date that will live in infamy" in his speech to Congress. Overnight, he managed to pull together a nation that had been divided and near-isolationist. But even though his speech rang with the force of immediacy, Roosevelt had begun to prepare for such a moment long before. Two years earlier, as war broke out in Europe, he had already mobilized American materiel by granting the British Royal Navy use of American destroyers. His planning for such a contingency was well underway—and so he was able to respond to a surprise attack.

"Today is the Pearl Harbor of this generation," said George W. Bush, after the terrorist strikes on September 11, 2001, as smoke hung on the horizons in Washington and New York. It was not the first attack against Americans in recent memory, but the others—the World Trade Center bombing in 1993; the Khobar Towers in Saudi Arabia in 1996; the U.S. embassies in East Africa in 1998; the USS *Cole* in 2000—had failed to rally us. A CIA intercept spoke of a bold attack referring to "Hiroshima in America." Despite the warnings, the attacks of September 11 came in a way no one envisioned. While zigzagging back to the White House to face the crisis, President Bush spoke to the nation from an air base in Louisiana. Though stumbling over a word or two he emphatically concluded: "The resolve of our great nation is being tested. But make no mistake: We will show the world that we will pass

---

Warning and Decision, Thomas Schelling wrote, "If we think of the entire U.S. government and its far-flung military and diplomatic establishment, it is not true that we were caught napping at the time of Pearl Harbor. We just expected wrong. And it was not our warning that was most at fault, but our strategic analysis." Roberta Wohlstetter, *Pearl Harbor: Warning and Decision* (New York: Stanford University Press, 1962), p. vi.

this test." The words, and his appearance at Ground Zero two days later, with ashes still smoldering, emboldened and inspired the stunned and angry nation. Bush had acted decisively.

Hurricane Katrina proved to be Bush's second test in responding decisively to a crisis, but this time he failed. He flew over New Orleans instead of being on the ground as he had been at ground zero after September 11th. He was removed from the crisis as was evidenced when he commended the head of Federal Emergency Management Agency (FEMA), as that agency floundered in its rescue operations. This is a warning as to how quickly a President in a crisis can lose the credibility he builds up in a well handled, preceding crisis.

Action for the Next President

It is likely the next President, like Lincoln, Roosevelt, and Bush, will be tested by a catastrophic event early in his or her first term. Prime Minister Gordon Brown faced terrorist attacks in London and Glasgow only three days after assuming office, and performed well. Various terrorist networks will see the 2008-2009 Presidential transition as an opportunity to strike this country, too.

If such an attack occurs, the next President will be dramatically tested before the American people. In preparing for this possibility, the President should take advantage of the Top Officials exercise (TOPOFF) created to manage potential crises. As we know from the anthrax crisis in the wake of September 11, clear communication with the public is crucial. In addition to the President and Homeland Security Secretary, it might be wise to convince a retired network news anchor such as Tom Brokaw to be trained and temporarily used as a crisis spokesman. In addition, the Department of Homeland Security overlap of outgoing and incoming officials is essential to maintaining a stable unit. But he or she should also look beyond the near term, and work to put in place a program that will allow future Presidents and leaders to call effectively on the determination and public spiritedness of Americans in the wake of an attack, or natural disaster.[*]

A major vulnerability exacerbates the looming threat of a terrorist attack during the Presidential transition. At this time, no Department or Agency of the U.S. government is clearly responsible or accountable for immediate disaster management following the detonation of a nuclear weapon or an improvised nuclear device on American soil.[**]

In the years following Hurricane Katrina, when the world watched as implementation of the newly crafted National

---

[*] This is a conclusion resulting from a meeting of the Preventive Defense Project on April 19, 2007, codirected by Dr. Ashton Carter of Harvard University and Dr. William Perry of Stanford University. Participants included General John Abizaid, former Commander of U.S. Central Command; Dr. Michael Anastasio, Director, Los Alamos National Laboratory; General James Cartwright, Commander of U.S. Strategic Command; Dr. Vahid Majidi, Assistant Director, Weapons of Mass Destruction, FBI; Dr. Gordon Oehler, former Director, Nonproliferation Center, CIA and Deputy Director, WMD Commission; and Dr. James Tegnelia, Director, Defense Threat Reduction Agency. Dr. Graham Allison, Director of the Belfer Center for Science and International Affairs at Harvard University and the leading analyst of U.S. National Security and Defense Policy, has warned repeatedly that the United States is gravely under-prepared for this threat.

[**] In its role as the host of a Nuclear Defense Working Group, composed of a range of top scientists and policymakers, Center for the Study of the Presidency staff were informed firsthand that there is no lead agency or department at the present time responsible in any way (legislated or otherwise) for the consequence management of a nuclear attack. However, the Domestic Nuclear Detection Office is working to extend its mandate of detection to include some form of response-capability, with very limited funding.

Response Plan failed at all levels, there has been little improvement made to the strategy. It has been renamed the National Response Framework, and now includes, as a supporting document, a set of fifteen planning scenarios, including both natural disasters and potential terrorist attacks.[1] Unfortunately, without prior coordination agreements and training between the agencies, the chaos created by a nuclear detonation will almost certainly overcome the management capabilities of any government authority. Explicit planning and articulation of the roles specific institutions will play in the event of a catastrophic event must occur, as well as training in the leadership skill sets that such disaster management requires.

What's more, the FEMA lacks the capability and training to respond to a nuclear attack. Consider an obvious scenario. In the event that first responders—police, fire, emergency, and other local services—are incapacitated in a nuclear attack due to radiation fall-out, victims will not receive any assistance for at least the first twenty-four hours. Furthermore, a nuclear attack on Washington will "decapitate" U.S. leadership.* Who would take over? In the midst of such chaos, there remains no single individual or organization assigned to manage this crisis.[2]

Only the next President has the ability to remedy this gaping vulnerability. He or she must consider creating a task force to investigate the best method for delineating the lines of each

---

* Fred Iklé, former Under Secretary of Defense for Policy, discussed how the Congress in particular has excessive optimism about U.S. technological progress that disregards the growing divergence between technology and the global political order. He notes that the Congress has also failed to pass legislation to determine restoration after a nuclear attack (see Fred Iklé, *Annihilation from Within: The Ultimate Threat to Nations* [New York: Columbia University Press, 2006]).

agency and departmental jurisdiction, including that of the United States military. Our armed forces are the most coordinated, well-trained federal entity to manage such a crisis, but military response must be tempered with the experience and capabilities of other agencies within departments such as Homeland Security and Energy.

Part of the problem is that at the White House level we have separate national security counsels and homeland security counsels, and therefore an inevitable division of labor. Our answer would be that the new Vice President should be charged with this role overarching these two White House entities.

CHAPTER 7

SETTING PRIORITIES

THROUGHOUT THE Civil War, Abraham Lincoln maintained a firm sense of priorities. When the Union Navy captured two Confederate diplomats en route to Britain on a British warship, the *Trent*, Westminster cried that their neutrality had been violated. Lincoln's Cabinet unanimously pushed for a declaration of war against England, but Lincoln silenced them: "One war at a time."

Like Lincoln, Franklin Roosevelt possessed an uncanny ability to set priorities. He knew that victory in the European theater had to come first. Despite protestations from General Douglas MacArthur and Admiral Chester Nimitz, the Pacific would come second. His Presidency spanned two very different national emergencies—the Depression and World War II—and his ability to prioritize during these events was fundamental to his success.

George W. Bush served at home during Vietnam as a Texas National Guard fighter pilot, and, like Lincoln, he had scant exposure to war before being thrust into the role of Commander-in-Chief. Like FDR, who emulated his cousin Theodore Roosevelt, George W. Bush had a model in his father, a young naval aviator in the Second World War, a war hero and the successful first Gulf War leader. But it is unclear that George W. Bush ever sought his father's advice. His father's National Security Advisor, Brent Scowcroft, was appointed as George W. Bush's chairman of the President's Foreign Intelligence Advisory Board for Bush's first term, but during that period the Board never met with the President, except when sworn in.

Bush failed to follow Lincoln's wise injunction: "One war at a time." He attacked Iraq before completing the U.S. victory in Afghanistan, capturing Osama bin Laden, eradicating al-Qaeda in the region, or completing reconstruction of that war-torn nation. As a result, U.S. forces have become stretched to the limit in both theaters. This strategic failure also left Pakistan vulnerable; a nation with nuclear weapons in radical hands would be devastating.

Many books have been written on the mismanagement of strategy, tactics, and reconstruction in Iraq,[1] but far less on Afghanistan, where the September 11th plot was conceived. It's undeniable that we've made numerous mistakes in the last seven years. Some of these were, perhaps, unavoidable, but others not. The first mistake that was made while setting strategic priorities was the President's loss of focus on finding Osama bin Laden and his premature pulling of forces from Afghanistan, before the mission was completed.

A second failure lay in not giving priority to mobilizing the twenty-six members of the NATO alliance, something which had been essential in winning the Cold War. Immediately after September 11th, NATO, led by European members, voted to invoke Article 5 of the Alliance charter, stipulating that an attack on any NATO member was an attack on them all. In response, our leaders offered the back of the hand. Caught in a unilateral mentality, we sought "coalitions of the willing" rather than genuine multilateral partnerships. (Both could have been utilized.) With successful experiences in the Balkans in the 1990s, NATO was a perfect resource to utilize. It was finally and belatedly in 2003 that the administration asked NATO to move peacekeeping forces into parts of Northern Afghanistan, only after the resurgent Taliban began to reconstitute themselves from safe havens in Pakistan, along with al-Qaeda. In 2005, NATO was asked to take over in Southern Afghanistan for what was called "peacekeeping" that more realistically constituted a mission of war—fighting to deal with a resurgent Taliban and well entrenched drug lords. The basic failure in priorities is repeated in the fact that our monthly investment in Iraq is $10 billion a month and $2 billion a month in Afghanistan.

A third misfire of the administration's campaign relates to India and Pakistan. In recent years we have developed open trade relations with India and a generous nuclear technology sharing policy. With Pakistan, on the other hand, there was no focus on cooperation and defining common goals. While Pakistan has proved a valuable player in the war in Afghanistan to some extent, the Pakistani government—though recipient of billions of dollars of economic and military aid—has not done enough to counteract the still-expanding safe haven for al-Qaeda in Northwest Pakistan, and furthermore as an army composed of large amounts of Pashton and Punjabi ethnic groups.

> As Eisenhower faced the long cold conflict with the Soviet Union, so we today face the prospect of a long war against terrorism

These setbacks resulting from a failure to set priorities illustrate how far we have slipped from the careful prioritization of Lincoln and Roosevelt. Our next President must learn from these mistakes to succeed in the art of statecraft.

Action for the Next President

One of the first things the next President must do after assuming office is to lead a comprehensive review of various methods for defeating or, at a minimum, containing, global terrorism. Such an assessment is long overdue. Luckily, however, past Presidents offer instructive examples of how to effectively reorient national strategy in the face of new and unfolding threats. The sources and shapes of the threats are new, but the strategic thinking in encountering them is still relevant.

One of the most famous comprehensive reviews was the "Project Solarium" conducted by President Dwight Eisenhower in 1953 to evaluate, and explore alternatives to containment, which since 1947 had been the bedrock of American Cold War strategy. From the moment he took office, Ike knew that the global order was changing—Joseph Stalin was dead, the United States had entered a war in Korea, and Soviets were consolidating their control over Eastern Europe. The understood American strategy would also need to change, or at least adapt.

President Eisenhower decided to assign three teams of foreign policy experts to explore and defend rival international strategies: Team "A" would make the case for containment, Team "B" for a more aggressive variation of containment, and team "C" for "roll-back," the idea that military force should be used to "rollback" Soviet influence in countries where it had already taken root. This competitive method of policy assessment offered a thorough and rigorous analysis of the options at hand. At the end of each group's presentation, Eisenhower masterfully summarized the similarities and differences among the competing view, and closed with a sharp-eyed assessment of the direction national strategy would have to take. George Kennan—who at first had dismissed Eisenhower as a bullish army man and anti-intellectual—praised the Commanders-in-Chief "intellectual ascendancy over every man in the room. . . . He had such a mastery over the military issues involved."[2] While the containment policy emerged on top, the Solarium exercise helped Eisenhower and his advisors to amend and implement it more effectively. As Eisenhower faced the long cold conflict with the Soviet Union, so we today face the prospect of a long war against terrorism. While our strategic thinking still lags behind that of Eisenhower's generation—it would be difficult to identify a counterterrorism strategy with the credibility of Kennan's containment, if only because the nature of the enemy is so diffused and shifting—a Solarium-like framework remains a tremendously effective tool for understanding and formulating the nation's foreign policy priorities. The next President should assign teams to assess and issue recommendations regarding America's military, diplomatic, financial, and political challenges related to the threat of Islamic fundamentalism. A second phase could further hone American strategy by offering concrete strategy recommendations in the manner of Eisenhower's teams "A," "B," and "C."

Such a process would be crucial for allowing strategy-makers a chance to rise above the day-to-day considerations of near-term challenges. It would also lend credibility to whichever strategy framework was eventually decided upon. Finally, it would further reinforce a precedent of constructive competition and an open decision-making process.

CHAPTER 8

MOBILIZING RESOURCES

I N THE WAKE of Fort Sumter, Abraham Lincoln not only called up 75,000 volunteers; he assumed control of the telegraph and the railway systems in the North, turned them into instruments of war, and energized the Northern industrial machine that would ultimately crush the poorer agrarian South. When he saw that it would take a long, costly war to save the Union, he pushed through a draft program that mobilized 300,000 more men for the army.

Franklin Roosevelt organized a wartime economy that ultimately overwhelmed the Axis powers. He directed the Bureau of the Budget to strengthen its professional management staff under the able direction of Donald Stone, who assisted the White House in creating the new war agencies. Roosevelt was confronted with conflicts, strikes, bottlenecks, and disorganization on the domestic front, due to uncoordinated economic policies and misallocations of people and resources. He responded by persuading a powerful, politically shrewd former Senator and Supreme Court Justice, James Byrnes of South Carolina, to be his war economy czar. Sewell Avery, the former CEO of Sears Roebuck and a captain of American industry, supervised war production, while Byrnes oversaw price controls. Other prominent Republicans were put to work. Classifying Byrnes's authority, Roosevelt told him: "Your decision is final and there is no appeal."[1] Roosevelt knew how to delegate, and how to draw out his delegate's particular talent.

Even before the war, Roosevelt had created the National Defense Research Committee under the outstanding scientist-engineer Vannevar Bush. Bush mobilized the research universities and national laboratories while borrowing from pioneering British researchers to further develop radar, the proximity fuse, and antisubmarine technologies.

In a letter from Albert Einstein in early August 1938, FDR learned that the Germans might have been developing an atomic bomb. He responded by marshaling the country's scientific genius—drawing on the immense brainpower that had come to the country seeking asylum from tyranny and persecution. In 1941, he created the Manhattan Project under Brigadier General Leslie Groves. It was housed at the University of Chicago, then Hanford, Washington, then Oak Ridge, Tennessee, and finally the Los Alamos Laboratory, and was led by Robert Oppenheimer. In four short years, U.S. physicists were able to build the atomic bomb. We have lost this historic ability to mobilize the nation's industrial and technological intellect for success.

In November of 2002, following a Congressional initiative pioneered by Senator Joe Lieberman, the administration moved to set up the Department of Homeland Security (DHS) with the enormous task of synergizing twenty-two agencies into one department. Former Governor Tom Ridge became the first Secretary in charge of this Herculean task.

One particular triumph of coordination could stand as a model for future DHS projects: Both Ridge and his successor, Michael Chertoff, are to be commended on supporting action to meet our single most important threat—that of smuggled nuclear weapons detonated in a major U.S. city. As a result of an outside Task Force (under the auspices of the 2005 Center for the Study of the Presidency Round Table Series) that gathered representatives from the National Laboratories, Department of

Energy, and DHS, chaired by Nor-
man Augustine and then Deputy
Secretary Admiral James Loy, DHS
moved rapidly to set up a Domestic
Nuclear Detection Office (DNDO)
with half a billion dollars this past
year.* The DNDO initiative is a
model private-public partnership. It
involves developing the before-men-
tioned layered defense against smug-
gled nuclear weapons or materials, and
it also greatly increases investment in
transformational research for both public and private laboratories.

> **Effective solutions come from harnessing the competitive spirit and creativity of the private sector with the organization and funding of the government.**

On the larger home front, the last five years of combat in
Afghanistan and Iraq have re-created failures of the Vietnam
experience, with our inability to mobilize the home front for
success (or what some would term "victory") including shared
sacrifice by our citizenry. The lack of synergies among our
various departments in the Iraq effort was first noted by the

---

* In this special task force hosted at the Center from 2004-2005,
the participants agreed that upon establishment of the DNDO, cur-
rent technology fell far short of what was needed to provide a sig-
nificant defense against the threat of smuggled nuclear weapons,
especially in light of the ease of shielding nuclear material. Working
group members co-chaired by Admiral James Loy and Norm Augus-
tine, including Fred Iklé, Robert Joseph, Richard Mies, James Abra-
hamson, Michael Carter, Henry Cooper, and Richard Wagner. To
achieve widespread surveillance of U.S. borders, DNDO needed
detectors that were inexpensive and autonomous, capable of demon-
strating competent selectivity and sensitivity, and manufactured in
large numbers. While such capabilities were beyond current tech-
nology, these goals were not beyond the limits of physics. Achieving
these goals would require a long-term national R&D commitment
pursued in conjunction with universities and private industry.

Government Accountability Office, and next by the then chairman of the Senate Armed Services Committee, Senator John Warner, who then wrote a letter of chastisement to the Department Secretaries.

President George W. Bush has belatedly appointed Lieutenant General Douglas Lute as "war czar" to coordinate efforts on Iraq and Afghanistan. He is to oversee the coordination and mobilization of the Executive branch in Washington to support our commanders and senior diplomats on the ground in Iraq and Afghanistan. But his appointment came a full seven months after the Baker-Hamilton Iraq Study Group laid out this recommendation, and it hardly reflects the adroit delegating that allowed FDR to select the great war leaders of midcentury America.[2]

Action for the Next President

For homeland defense, the larger project of erecting layered defenses for smuggled weapons of mass effect will take time, but must be confronted by the next President with more vigor than before.* The task of bringing together operations from dozens of government agencies within the Department of Homeland Security—each with their own mandates and factional traditions

---

* In 2005, the Secretary of Homeland Security charged his Homeland Security Advisory Council to establish a task force on "Preventing the Entry of Weapons of Mass Effect Into the United States," composed of Council members and government representatives. Foremost, the task force identified critical deficiencies in the current state of WME prevention, specifically noting the absence of a systematic, risk-based approach to investment; dispersed capabilities in leadership and decision-making; inadequate attention to engaging foreign partners; deterrence concepts in need of update; need for greater urgency and priority for investments in technological innovation; and lack of citizen engagement.

and rivalries—is no easy task. The President should take the advice of current and former CEOs who have managed significant, successful corporate mergers, such as Lockheed Martin, Procter and Gamble, General Electric, Microsoft, and Google. The Toyota method of "quality circles"—teams of creative thinkers who cut across compartmentalization—should be employed within the agencies of Homeland Security.

Many of the assumptions that underpin the modern national security establishment are no longer valid and a complete reevaluation of our armed services, National Guard, and reserves must be carried out by our next President. This must include how these establishments are integrated with other government agencies to achieve unity of effort. Nothing can substitute for good leadership, but even with the best leadership many of the failures in execution in Iraq and Afghanistan would have been unavoidable and are symptomatic of larger systemic failure.

> **The findings of the Project for Nation Security Reform give the next President a valuable head start.**

The findings of the Project for National Security Reform, whose aims include the update and broadening of the National Security Act, will aid the next President enormously and give him or her a valuable head start in creating a new set of tools for the challenges of a new era. The Goldwater-Nichols Act gave incentive to joint command and staff service for career military officers, making possible the jointness that won the Gulf War. It was the lack of such incentive that made it so difficult to have personnel from

---

The panel was chaired by Lydia Thomas of Mitretek Systems, and Jared Cohon, of Carnegie Mellon University, the three subgroups focusing on WME entry by air, land, and sea, were respectively led by Norman Augustine, James Schlesinger, and myself.

the Departments of Agriculture and Health and Human Services, to serve in Provincial Reconstruction teams in Iraq. Congressional leadership must be deeply involved throughout this process, as national security reform cuts across numerous Congressional committees and interests. To be successful, national security reform will require bipartisan commitment and a high degree of coordination.

With regard to the armed services, the new Commander-in-Chief must recognize the importance of both the morale and creativity of the military. Part of this renewal will involve a re-strengthening of military educational institutions, ranging from the service academies and ROTC to the War Colleges. One problem we face is in retention rates. Out of the 903 officers commissioned at West Point in 2001, nearly 46 percent left the service last year, and more than 54 percent of the class of 2000 left by January 2007.[3]

Another challenge involves a restrengthening of military educational institutions, ranging from the service academies and ROTC to the War Colleges. Even during the years between the First and Second World Wars, when our military was neglected, we managed to maintain a strong military-sponsored educational system. That system prepared the generals and admirals to become the strategic thinkers and commanders who won World War II. Today, the War Colleges struggle to attract the most promising officers. The military institutions are underfunded and this issue is partly the fault of the Congress. Of course, the military academies have alumni who did not pursue a military career but contributed to national security formulation in Cabinet and sub-Cabinet positions.

The division between civilians and military in the national security complex can be overemphasized. The next administration needs to improve the civil-military relationship. Donald Rumsfeld's controversial legacy as Secretary of Defense, like Robert McNamara's, has been the subject of numerous critical books and articles.* Of course, the Founding Fathers sought to guard against an Oliver Cromwell or even a Duke of Marlborough. Though not the head of government, Marlborough, as a brilliant general, led Britain into continental wars beyond national interests. This example was in the minds of the Founders as they sought to ensure civilian authority over the military. Furthermore, they realized that war was—as Clausewitz later wrote—"a continuation of politics by other means."[4]

The issue is not this principle of ultimate civilian direction, but how to obtain a better balance in the civil military relationship. This balance is needed to obtain the most creative military advice, recognizing that the military do not always agree with each other. It has been argued that we have lacked that balance recently, at least until Secretary Robert M. Gates took over the Defense Department.** In 2002, Eliot Cohen published a book called

---

*Upon entering office, Secretary Rumsfeld drove the military revolution ruthlessly against the obstacles of the acquisition process. Using the products of this revolution, conventional phases of the Afghan and Iraq wars were well fought, it was in the follow up phases where the disaster occurred. As for the revolution in military affairs, one center of creativity, the Pentagon, which Rumsfeld maintained, is office of net assessments, headed by Andrew Marshall. This office was instituted by strategic minded sec of defense James Schlesinger and maintains a network into the think tank world.

** The civil-military relationship is explored more fully in Colonel H. R. McMaster's book, widely read in the military, *Dereliction of Duty: Lyndon Johnson, Robert McNamara, the Joint Chiefs of Staff, and the Lies that Led to Vietnam* (New York: HarperCollins, 1997). One of its theses is that the Joint Chiefs should have spoken up more forcefully in private to their superiors and in Congressional testimony and to correct Congressional misinterpretations of their views. This book intensified the debate about the appropriate relationship between civilians and the military, and, since the United States launched wars in Afghanistan and Iraq, this debate

Supreme Command,[5] read by President Bush. Cohen selected Abraham Lincoln, Georges Clemenceau, Winston Churchill, and David Ben-Gurion, as case studies of heads of government who championed the importance of civilian control of the military, but went beyond this, giving specific direction of some military operations, thus overriding military judgments. This point struck a chord with the new Bush administration that believed the military had fallen out of control under the Clinton Administration. Rumsfeld was the man to right the imbalance. In light of the tremendous failures in the planning and execution of the Iraq War, Cohen's argument was misapplied. With regard to the Afghanistan and Iraq wars, our civilian war leaders lacked the talents and skills of Abraham Lincoln or Franklin Roosevelt. Indeed, the member of the Bush Cabinet with the most experience was former four-star general and combat veteran Secretary of State Colin Powell, who had been National Security Advisor under Ronald Reagan and later chairman of the Joint Chiefs of Staff during the Gulf War. Unfortunately, his advice on war planning was overruled by those without his level of experience.[*]

The necessary conclusion is that neither the military nor civilians are infallible, and it is therefore important to have a

---

is all the more timely. For more on this debate, see Michael Desch, "Bush and the Generals" *Foreign Affairs* (May/June 2007, 86:3, pp. 97–108), and subsequent responses, "Salute and Disobey?" *Foreign Affairs* (September/October 2007, 86:5, pp. 147–56).

[*]As for the Department of Defense, the arrival of Robert Gates resulted in an immediate change in the top-down culture. He brought with him the multidimensional leadership qualities that marked his tenure as president of Texas A&M University. Gates also had the advantage of serving eight months in the Iraq Study Group, as well as having a previous outstanding intelligence career. His scholarly book *From the Shadows: The Ultimate Insider's Story of Five Presidents and How They Won the Cold War* (New York: Simon and Schuster, 2007) was one of the best on the Cold War.

proper dynamic between the two in planning and executing wartime strategy and discussion of tactics and technology. It is also helpful to include those who have had previous military experience within the civilian leadership. Such a role was filled by two-time National Security Advisor Lt. General Brent Scowcroft and General Powell, not to mention Secretary of State George Marshall.

Fortunately, many of our recent military leaders have been highly educated. Two such examples are General John Abizaid, who has his Ph.D. in Middle Eastern Studies and speaks Arabic, and General David Petraeus, who was a member of the social science faculty at West Point after earning a Princeton Ph.D. The important requirement for the next President is to develop open and creative thinking throughout the national defense complex and to involve the War Colleges in the long-term debate.

Yet it is important to remember that even the most brilliant officers sometime cannot escape the consequences of the uncertainty that war brings. The "fog of war" leads some of the best plans to be shattered by "game changers"—unpredictable events that dramatically change the reality that the plans were based on. Three years ago General David Petraeus, the creator of the innovative *Counterinsurgency Field Manual* that transformed the army's operations in Iraq and Afghanistan, estimated that the reconstruction and rebuilding of Iraqi security forces was going on a steady path to progress and success.[6] His optimism and plans for further success had to be altered by a single event—the bombing of the Al-Askari Mosque—which resurfaced the threats of civil war in Iraq, a constant concern since that event. War is always plagued with the unanticipated, and in counterinsurgency compounded by civil war that plague accelerates. Still, these tactical battles must not stultify our leaders from thinking strategically about our larger interest.

President Eisenhower warned that this strategic initiative cannot be done by those directing daily operations. This requires highly adaptable strategies, and creative and strong leaders on both the military and civilian fronts that can carry those strategies forward. Such strategies provide the vision, framework, and overall purpose in which to carry out solid operational and tactical plans, such as those developed by General Petraeus, which are essential but cannot stand alone as a substitute for such strategies.

In our nation's history, the diversity of strategic challenges has never been as great as it is today. The threats range from counterinsurgency and dealing with non-state actors to adding stability to great power contests to security in space. Not only do new roles and missions of the military need to be reviewed but the joint commands need to be rethought as tools not merely of force but of power and influence. For example, the U.S. Navy uses carrier divisions throughout the Pacific to maintain a balance of power between Korea, Japan, and China. These "carriers in position," and in motion, have a huge political role. Then there is the threat of global terrorism and counterinsurgency. The Navy's reach and freedom of action must be maximized and amply demonstrated, particularly at a time when the Army, Marine Corps, and National Guard are tied down in the Middle East and elsewhere in addition to dealing with an incipient Civil War.

On the subject of power-projection, the new President needs to work with the military to reconceptualize what Secretary Rumsfeld has called the "Combatant Commanders." Rumsfeld coined the term to distinguish the commanders of joint Army, Navy, Marine, Air Force, and State Department elements—formerly called CINCs—from the overall Commander-in-Chief, the President. But the very word "combatant" detracts from the CINCs primary role of molding the strategic environment using force only as a last resort, but often using its potential as an element of deterrence. Renaming the commanders with the aggressive title "combatant" completely misses the point that these commanders discern between power and force; utilizing their power and not their force.

Such military instruments can play a critical role in deterring enemies and enhancing regional stability. One major commander is simultaneously responsible as NATO commander and Supreme Allied Commander Europe (SACEUR). His prime role deals with the ideal of conflict prevention; including monitoring, enforcement, and peacekeeping operations. The Alliance responsibility means he operates not under the American but rather the NATO flag, providing us the advantage of more impartial involvement.

As we face these challenges of reform and renewal, the new Administration should re-create the dynamism of the Joint Chiefs of Staff, which thrived in the 1990s for several reasons. First of all, Senator John Warner imposed a request for net assessments, forcing the services to work together. Second, Chairman of the Joint Chiefs of Staff General John Shalikashvili, and his extraordinary Vice Chief Admiral Bill Owens, published a report in 1996 that stretched strategic thinking toward military capabilities in the year 2010.[7] At the same time, there were advances in "network centric" warfare, which interlinks computer technology on the battlefield, providing commanders with real time access to battlefield information. Third, the effects of the Goldwater-Nichols legislation had taken effect, requiring joint staff service as well as command duty for promotion. Thus the Joint Staff became filled with dynamic talent.

The next President should restore this creativity to the Joint Staff.

In the First and Second World Wars, as well as the Cold War, our alliances were magnifiers of our

> ∽ **In the First and Second World Wars, as well as the Cold War, our alliances were magnifiers of our power**

power, especially since we were consistently the leaders of the alliances. How does the next President look beyond our shores, and reprioritize our commitments to alliances, while working to reform those alliances? A first focus should be on the NATO alliance, which served us so decisively in the Cold War victory. Over time, NATO has expanded to forty-six members including partners, or associate allies. It has gone through remarkable transformations and now bears a major role in Afghanistan, as it did in the Balkan conflicts.

Outgoing SACEUR General James Jones argues that NATO's bureaucratic process could be easily trimmed: all that is needed is a change in procedures that requires consensus and decision-making only at the top body but not throughout the numerous subsidiary bodies at NATO.* Second, NATO, like our Department of Defense, is involved in tasks of reconstruction where it is not fully equipped. In many cases, the European Union (EU) has greater capabilities. As we draw down our forces in Iraq, the United States must solicit key European nations in a major new initiative to rally publics and parliaments behind a greater commitment for success in Afghanistan. An effort should be made to develop far more crosswalks between NATO and the EU as well as a joint command or task force on reconstruction.

At the same time, the next President should take initiative in the United Nations to develop greater capabilities for peace-keeping in cooperation with other organizations, such as dealing with the crises in Darfur. In addition, we have a major new opportunity to make France an ally in these new initiatives

---

* Specifically, this means consensus throughout the Atlantic Council's various forms: heads of government, foreign and defense ministers, and permanent representatives. The subsidiary bodies would perform by majority vote or perhaps representative vote depending upon the degree of national investment.

under the leadership of Nicholas Sarkozy.* In the Northern Pacific, perhaps the six-power talks over North Korea could evolve into a five-power North Asian consulting group. Meanwhile, the stabilizing U.S. Japanese treaty relationship must remain vibrant.

As we shore up American power abroad, we must not forget domestic investments—particularly in the fields of science, technology and communications. Here again we can refer to Lincoln and Roosevelt, who realized that such investments affect the nation's destiny in unforeseen ways. Successful solutions come from harnessing the competitive spirit and creativity of the private sector with the organization and funding of the government. Recently, however, government and business alike have failed to adequately fund basic scientific research— a wellspring of American innovation. Since 1993, even Pentagon funding of basic research has declined by 10 percent according to a National Research Council Report.[8] We tend to forget that many of our most dynamic developments in the

---

*Along these lines, in late 2004 Congressman Frank Wolf sponsored legislation that established the bipartisan Task Force on the United Nations, cochaired by former Speaker of the House Newt Gingrich and former Senate Majority Leader George Mitchell. The United States Institute of Peace was charged with overseeing the organization of the Task Force and its efforts. The Task Force report, entitled "American Interests and UN Reform," was issued in June 2005. Its findings and recommendations, which received wide praise, addressed the urgent need for reforms at the United Nations, in such areas as management and accountability, safeguarding human rights and ending genocide, conflict prevention and peacekeeping, and deterring the proliferation of weapons of mass destruction and combating terrorism. In the report, Speaker Gingrich and Senator Mitchell emphasized that "a strong and effective United Nations can be an important instrument for the pursuit of the American goals of freedom and security."

civilian economy, such as the Internet and the Global Positioning System, emerged from military research and development.

Meanwhile, powerful new global competitors led by China, India, and others are staking claims to the future. The next President will confront a potential decline in the nation's global technological standing and a range of technology-based problems that deserve attention at the highest levels of government. Presidential leadership to address such challenges as homeland security, climate change, health care, energy security, and economic growth will require access to sound scientific assessments and the nation's preeminent technological resources.[*]

---

[*] Many of our Presidential candidates have realized this urgency. By the summer of 2007, leading Republican and Democratic candidates alike had indicated their views related to science and technology policy issues such as funding for research and development, stem cell research and science and mathematics education. Rudy Giuliani, as mayor of New York City, had been a strong supporter of increasing investment in biomedical research and proponent of the economic value of technological progress. Former Massachusetts Governor Mitt Romney had called for increased funding for emerging technologies stating, "It is time to invest substantially in technologies related to power generation, nanotechnology, and materials science." Neither, however, had made definitive statements on stem cell research. On the Democratic side, both Senators Barack Obama and Hillary Clinton had stated their support for embryonic stem cell research. On strengthening the nation's innovative capacity, Senator Obama had endorsed initiatives to increase the participation of women and underrepresented minorities in the professions of science, technology, engineering, and mathematics and Senator Clinton had unveiled a comprehensive nine-point "Innovation Agenda" that included calls for increased funding for research and development in mission agencies, a permanent research and experimentation (R&E) tax credit for the private sector, and decreased politicization of federal science policy.

Notwithstanding this emphasis on science, there is still no substitute for manpower, shared national sacrifice, and especially "youth power" in the defense of our homeland— our states, cities, and towns. Today, in some states, 15 percent or more of our National Guard are deployed overseas, leaving us exposed to terrorist attack or natural disaster at home. But there is a deep well of patriotic young adults who care

∞ **But there is a deep well of patriotic young adults who care about America and about protecting their communities from terrorism and disaster**

about America and about protecting their communities from terrorism and disaster, who would gladly sacrifice to make their communities safer places. Alexis de Tocqueville in the 1830s noted that by nature America is a nation of joiners. We should give youth this opportunity to join in the protection of their communities. This would be the first clear call for shared sacrifice since the efforts immediately following September 11th.

The new President should reiterate this call by encouraging nationwide participation in a community-based "Home Guard" program. This would echo President John Kennedy's inaugural call, "Ask not what your country can do for you, but what you can do for your country." This initiative should be funded through the Department of Homeland Security, but also harness the leadership abilities of governors and local governments throughout our nation. This Home Guard would be composed of volunteers from communities who would help defend those communities, and would train on weekends in uniform with the National Guard and first responders such as fire, police, EMS, the Red Cross, and NGOs. Directed especially at youth, the program should encourage older persons with special skill sets to join, too. This group would perform duties in support of the National

Guard or Reserves, but in a nonex-
peditionary function, and hence
would have access to a wide range
of young people that might not sign
up for the military forces deployable
overseas. In addition to training,
there could be a G.I. Bill program for education of young peo-
ple in order to provide incentives to join.*

> ∾ **Educated youth is the backbone of our national power**

Educated youth is the backbone of our national power. A
more robust early education system must be part of the
national security agenda. Former Speaker of the House Newt
Gingrich was largely responsible for setting up the United
States Commission on National Security in the twenty-first
century in 1998. Well before 9/11, it perceived that the great-
est single threat to American security was a terrorist nuclear
attack on the homeland. The second greatest threat, however,
was the nation's "failures in math and science education." Gin-
grich has bemoaned the fact that the Commission's warnings
essentially repeated those made a full eighteen years earlier,
during the Reagan Administration (in its report *A Nation at
Risk: The Imperative of Educational Reform*).[9] The next Presi-
dent should increase funding at the K-12 level in the fields of
math and science. The new initiative should analyze past Pres-
idential projects and build upon the successful ones, including
the No Child Left Behind Act.

---

* Beginning in 2004, the Center for the Study of the Presidency
hosted a study group to discuss the concept of a nonexpeditionary
Home Guard. Participants included Albert C. Zapanta, Adjutant
Major General Claude A. Williams, Adjutant Maj. Gen. Jessica L.
Wright, Reginald Brown, Jeffrey Gaynor, Jack Marsh, General Shy
Meyer, Gen. Robert F. Ensselin, Dr. Charles Moskos, Lawrence
Korb, Brigadier General Richard Behrenhausen, LTG Theodore
Stroup Jr., General David Harris, General Daniel W. Christman,
and William A. Navas Jr.

Fortunately there is help to be had in the many civic and nonprofit institutions that thrive in our free society. For example, two of the country's leading education philanthropists, Eli Broad and Bill Gates, recently launched the "Strong American Schools" campaign, which can be an enormous resource for the next President to invest both personal and political capital in meeting America's K-12 educational challenges. The initiative urges candidates to address three common-sense priorities that hold tremendous promise for improving education: improving American educational standards, employing effective teachers in every classroom, and providing more time and support for in-depth learning and greater personal attention.[10] Equally important is the need to include character education, which has already found a range of public and private initiatives across the country. As for higher education, we do have the finest, but costs are becoming prohibitive, and that issue must be faced, perhaps within a conference of leading college educators called by the President.

Above all, the next President would be wise to emulate Thomas Jefferson, Abraham Lincoln, Franklin Roosevelt, and Dwight Eisenhower and take a comprehensive nationwide approach to mobilizing resources by incorporating research, education, science, and discovery as integral parts of our national power. There are numerous recent initiatives, which, as we have attempted to show, can provide models for future efforts.

CHAPTER 9

MAINTAINING POLITICAL UNITY AND SHREWD TIMING

D URING THE Civil War, Abraham Lincoln did everything he could to hold the country together. He denounced slavery, but he also insisted that the war was not being fought to abolish slavery but to prevent the illegal act of secession. This drew criticism from some of his Abolitionist allies, who called Lincoln hypocritical for turning against his "House Divided" theme. But Lincoln saw that the Civil War would be long and catastrophic, and so made many tactical concessions to keep the Northern effort together. He realized the need to maintain a coalition between the Northern and Border States, where slavery was widely practiced. Many in Tennessee, Kentucky, and Maryland would not fight a war "against slavery."

When the war changed, so did Lincoln. After the costly Union victory at Antietam in July 1862, Lincoln judged the time was right to radically expand the basis of the war. This masterful grand strategist conceived the Emancipation Proclamation to achieve a moral as well as tactical reversal. And it was issued with care: Lincoln warned the nation six months in advance. As he promised, in January 1863, he issued the Emancipation Proclamation, ending slavery in the Confederacy, but not in the loyal North. This move gave him the highest moral ground and benefited the North advantageously: in Europe, it discouraged the threat of European recognition of the Confederacy. It also enabled Lincoln to recruit 180,000 African American troops, mobilize freed slaves leaving the South, and provide much needed idealistic and moral motivation for the Union war effort. And it helped transform the very character of the nation, as a country now committed to fulfill its own ideals of freedom. With the stroke of a pen, Lincoln commenced a second American Revolution. But it couldn't have been rushed. Two years earlier, the country would not have been ready for such a move. Lincoln had foresight and patience—two crucial traits that are often in short supply.

> ⁓ **The first step to restore our nation's confidence must be to ensure that the long-term strategic planning for the war on terror is inclusive and bipartisan.**

Seventy-eight years later, President Franklin Roosevelt used masterful timing to maintain unity as he reversed the policy of isolationism and mobilized and unified the nation for war. He was far ahead of the public and Congress in recognizing the long-term threat that Adolf Hitler posed, in his covert as well as public efforts to help an embattled England. Even before Japan's attack on Pearl Harbor in December 1941, Roosevelt created a bipartisan cabinet by appointing two prominent Republicans, Henry Stimson and Frank Knox, to head the War and Navy Departments, respectively. He sent his 1940 Presidential opponent, Republican Governor Wendell Willkie, to England as his special envoy to Winston Churchill. As a war leader, FDR knew that the national interest superseded party interests.

George W. Bush came to the Presidency in the shadow of a disputed election, the first since 1876. Before all of his political appointees were confirmed, terrorists attacked the World Trade Center and the Pentagon. That night, the President publicly announced a pillar of what would become the Bush Doctrine: "We will make no distinction between the terrorists who committed these acts and those who harbor them." Understanding that it would be critical to avoid the appearance of a war between the West and Islam, Bush quickly visited a Washington mosque and declared that Osama bin Laden was distorting a great religion. He praised Muslim Americans and avoided any repetition of xenophobic anti-Japanese emotional antagonisms and actions at the beginning of World War II. The President also reached out with a deft combination of pressure and diplomacy to Islamic countries as partners in the antiterror coalition.

Shortly after the attacks, Bush went to Capitol Hill, gave a rousing, unifying speech, and embraced the Democratic Senate Majority Leader and the House Minority Leader. For the first three months after September 11, Bush's leadership held the nation and the world in confidence. In less than a decade, this confidence has been lost as the nation has polarized over the Iraq War and America's image has dramatically deteriorated abroad.

The next President must remember to be the leader of the entire country, not only his party, and that great minds and patriotic hearts exist across the political spectrum and in every state.

Action for the Next President

How can the next President restore this confidence? The first step must be ensuring that the long-term strategic planning for the war on terror is inclusive and bipartisan. The Solarium-like exercise mentioned in the section above should include thinkers and leaders from both parties. He or she must also reach out to the best minds from outside of Washington—to labs, universities, and journalists knowledgeable in the defense and foreign policy fields. The next President must remember to be the leader of the entire country, not only his party, and that great minds and patriotic hearts exist across the political spectrum and in every state.

For both Abraham Lincoln and Franklin Roosevelt, the first objective of their wartime cabinets was to unify the country. As party leader, the new President must convince that party that it will serve its political interests best by serving the national interest at this time of severe challenges at home and abroad. A "unity cabinet" would help in this regard. There have been examples of this unity. As war approached, President Roosevelt brought onboard Secretary of War, Henry L. Stimson (Herbert Hoover's former Secretary of State) along with Frank Knox as Secretary of the Navy, who ran against the FDR ticket as Vice President in 1936. John F. Kennedy selected Republican Douglas Dillon as Secretary of the Treasury and later John McCone as his Director of CIA. Above all, the next President must seek to keep the nation's trust and be assured that the new Cabinet members seek to do the same. The new Vice President must be someone possessing the skills and talents to make the national security system work in harmony, and must also be committed to building partnerships with Congress.

There was another important role for the Vice President that the Center for the Study of the Presidency made during the 2000 government transition. We suggested the Vice President chair a national, nonpartisan coalition of America's most talented private sector leaders within the various fields that should make up the diverse components of our grand strategy. Vice President elect, Dick Cheney, to his credit, agreed in principle to this idea, but after the attacks of September 11, 2001, it went by the wayside.

We recommend that the next President take up this initiative again, drawing from the 2001 CSP report *Comprehensive Strategic Reform*.[1]

CHAPTER 10

COMMUNICATING AN UNDERSTANDABLE PUBLIC STRATEGY

THE PRESIDENT elected in 2008 will become not only the country's Commander-in-Chief but also the Communicator-in-Chief. In the Information Age, the actions, words, and policies of the President have a wider and more scrutinizing audience—not only among governments, but also among average people around the world—than ever before. Our failures in Iraq and exploding anti-American sentiment throughout the Middle East underscore the challenge and importance of rehabilitating the nation's reputation. Enormous damage has been done by the Abu Ghraib images replayed thousands of times on international television and our domestic debates over the issue of torture. This combat veteran would join with more distinguished ones such as Generals Colin Powell and P. X. Kelly, along with prisoner of war, Senator John McCain, who warn that we are losing the high moral ground.[1] That high ground is a critical dimension of U.S. power.

We ought to return to the most successful expressions of the American ideal—as an experiment in liberty, equality, and decency that offers hope for the world. To restore the American ideal, it will take a revolution in the way we understand and communicate the "better angels" of our nation's image. Diplomacy places primary emphasis on the pathways of official power—diplomats, summit meetings, communiqués and leader-to-leader consultations. What is called "public diplomacy" includes invaluable government funded cultural and educational exchanges (such as the Fulbright Scholarships), public affairs officers in embassies, and an array of government-sponsored international broadcasting under the auspices of the Broadcasting Board of

> Now more than ever, we need "public strategy" that is similarly accessible—not only to the citizens of this country, but to people around the world.

Governors. These components remain vitally important, but they no longer constitute the only levers of international influence. As Thomas Friedman has pointed out in *The World Is Flat*, the channels of international communication are changing fast.[2]

These new challenges require us to go far beyond the older but essential concepts of public diplomacy to create what we can call a "public strategy," that is, a strategy for our publics to communicate with other publics around the world.* Such a strategy—like all strategy—requires an artistic balancing or ends and means. But a public strategy will need to be more, because it must be rooted in the moral concepts that make America what it is. It also must overarch the numerous private sector channels—television, the Internet, international busi-

---

* In the mid-1950s, the famed columnist Walter Lippmann wrote a book called *Essays in Public Philosophy* (Boston: Little, Brown, 1955), in which he argued for enlightening all Americans in the essential precepts of the American creed. Writing in an age which, like ours, saw the proliferation of various communications media, he saw that American interests would be shaped not only by the actions of government but also by the judgments of peoples at home and abroad.

ness, NGOs, etc.—through which men and women around the world develop their judgments about American strengths, weaknesses, virtues, and vices.

The most important ingredients in our public strategy can be found in the country's founding documents. With the Declaration of Independence, we articulated a unique project of government based on the proposition that all men are created equal. At the same time we declared our need for a "decent respect for the opinions of mankind." The Constitution posited that a slave was only 3/5 of person, contradicting the equality proposition in a fundamental way, but it also laid out a practical pathway for realizing the bold claims of the Declaration. In the early 1790s, the *Federalist Papers*—first published in American newspapers and shortly afterwards in Europe—elaborated on and critiqued the workings of the new government, while warning, for instance, against the excesses to which democracy is prone without an effective system of checks and balances.

Federalist Paper #51 noted that "If men were angels, no government would be necessary," but that ". . . the great difficulty lies in this: you must first enable the government to control the governed; and in the next place to control itself."[3] Authors Alexander Hamilton, John Jay, and James Madison, like most of the Founding Fathers, had studied the destruction of unrestrained democracy in Ancient Greece. They would live to see the excesses in the French Revolution, which led to the "Reign of Terror" and later dictatorship. These three documents furnish a remarkable tutorial for our public strategy message today, at home and abroad. They should have been reviewed by some of the architects of the invasion of Iraq who expected instant democracy after the fall of Saddam Hussein.

The great utterances of Abraham Lincoln and Franklin Roosevelt added to these public strategies. Lincoln declared a "new birth of freedom" from the ruins of civil war. He renewed the promise that "government of the people, for the people, and by the people shall not perish from the earth."[4] His legacy—of hope for a divided nation and a freer, more equal society—should be revived as a pillar of our public strategy today, for he completed the Second American Revolution.[*]

Roosevelt eloquently utilized the dominant communications technology of his day, the radio, with his regular fireside chats and weekly press conferences. His speech heralding "Four Freedoms" outlined his public strategy: freedom of speech and religion and from want and fear. These Freedoms were simple and elegant and powerful. Roosevelt's finger was on the pulse of the nation and the world. Though he died before the war ended, his manner—buoyant in public, shrewd behind the scenes—helped to give his vision of Four Freedoms an aura of destiny.

The building blocks of such a strategy, however, would not be complete without a transformational leader who emerged not from the White House, but from the pulpit. On August 28, 1963, from the steps of the Lincoln memorial, Martin Luther King Jr. spoke to the country while the world listened. He called upon America to live out the true meaning of its creed—that "all men are created equal"—and that people should "not be judged by the color of their skin but by the content of their character."[5] With President Lyndon Johnson and the Voting Rights Act, this concluded the third American Revolution. It also spoke to the world.

In the grim events of September 11, individuals from eighty-four different nationalities from around the world were

---

[*] James McPherson wrote, "Abraham Lincoln was not a Maximilian de Robespierre. No competitive leaders went to the guillotine. Yet the Civil War changed the United States as thoroughly as the French Revolution changed that country." James M. McPherson, *Abraham Lincoln and the Second Revolution* (New York: Oxford University Press, 1991), p. viii.

represented among the victims. The George W. Bush Administration faced a completely new challenge, unique to our time. In the months that followed, most of the world rallied behind us against this act of terrorism not only against America, but the world as we knew it. However, since that time America's stock has plummeted. The American drama, which Washington sought to so carefully script on the world stage, has taken numerous desultory and unfortunate turns.

In the grim events of September 11, individuals from eighty-four different nationalities from around the world were represented among the victims

Part of the new challenge was to address the Muslim world. Although the U.S. counterattack on al-Qaeda and the Taliban was widely supported, the protracted war in Iraq is largely reviled in the Muslim world. In President Bush's second term inaugural he forthrightly said,

> We have seen our vulnerability—and we have seen its deepest source. For as long as whole regions of the world simmer in resentment and tyranny, prone to ideologies that feed hatred and excuse murder, violence will gather and multiply in destructive power, and cross the most defended borders and raise a mortal threat. . . . The survival of liberty in our land increasingly depends on the success of liberty in other lands. The best hope for peace in our world is the expansion of freedom in all the world.[6]

Despite the President's inspiring words, recent years have opened a vast chasm between American and Muslim perceptions regarding U.S. values and intentions. Large majorities in the Islamic world believe that the United States is actively seeking to undermine Islam—and many even believe we are trying to spread Christianity in these regions.[7] Not only do overwhelming numbers in Europe and the Middle East view the U.S. government unfavorably, majorities in countries like Egypt and Morocco believe that there has *never* been a time in history when the United States has sought to promote the welfare of other countries.[8] Support for the U.S. War on Terror is dropping across the globe,[9] while majorities in Jordan, Egypt, Indonesia, and Turkey believe that Arabs were not responsible for the 9/11 attacks.[10] Even in the United States—where Muslim's are generally better integrated than they are in European societies—a full 26 percent of Muslims age 18 to 29 believe that suicide bombing can be justified.[11] The list of worrisome statistics goes on. And yet to a great extent we still lack the institutional and ideological tools to turn back these trends. If we are to find them, we don't need to look any further back than Bush's second inaugural, when he qualified his statements by saying "America will not impose our own style of government on the unwilling. Our goal instead is to help others find their own voice, obtain their own freedom and make their own way."

Action for the Next President

The next President will need a counselor, within the White House, to act as an architect of diplomatic public strategy. In 2003, I served on a Special Advisory Board chaired by Ambassador Ed Djerejian. In our report, *Changing Minds, Winning Peace: A New Strategic Direction for U.S. Public Diplomacy in the Arab and Muslim Worlds*,[12] we recommended that to compensate somewhat for the loss of United States Information Agency (USIA), the President should appoint a Special Counselor for Public Diplomacy, with direct access to the President and the ability to participate in National Security Council deliberations. The next President should implement this advisory group's recommendation, but with an ever larger mandate.

Most of the recommendations of the Djerejian Report have been carried out by Undersecretary of State Karen Hughes. Her deputy, Dina Habib Powell, has also instituted an outstanding public-private partnership with U.S. business. As societies become more interconnected and corporations, NGOs, and individuals increasingly take on the responsibilities of unofficially representing America to non-Americans, public strategy will have to adapt. The next President in particular should recognize and promote public and private institutions that enhance American values and image abroad.

The development of the term two-track diplomacy gave total independence from government control, establishing a special unbiased credibility around the world. It is a necessity that diplomats practice *realpolitik* and deal successfully with nondemocratic countries. The second track of this diplomacy enabled our country and its public strategy to stand for its ideals while diplomatically pursuing self-interest. The Congress entered into two-track diplomacy by requiring the State Department to do an annual report on human rights in various countries worldwide. Foreign ambassadors of nondemocratic countries could protest vigorously to the Secretary of State, but this annual report was meeting a requirement of law over which the State Department has no control. As a part of our larger public strategy, outstanding NGOs have developed to promote conflict management and resolution including American Citizens Abroad, Seeds for Peace, and Search for Common Ground. Organizations such as the National Endowment for Democracy, the Republican and Democratic Institutes, and the United States Institute

> ⮑ **As FDR knew, American grand strategy must not be based on fear, but built from a clear set of priorities, the mobilization of national resources, and agility in the face of crisis.**

of Peace provide strong allies for these NGOs. The development of such initiatives grew out of Ronald Reagan's memorable Westminster Speech and was brought into action by a bipartisan coalition led by former Republican and Democratic Chairmen Bill Brock and Chuck Manatt.

Shortly after 9/11, Peter Peterson, Chairman of the Council on Foreign Relations, led a task force to identify ways of strengthening America's ability to communicate with other societies. Perhaps influenced by Peterson's wife, Joan Ganz Cooney, the creator of *Sesame Street*, the task force proposed the creation of an NGO that could mobilize private sector expertise to meet this challenge.

At the initiative of Congressman Frank Wolf, Congress subsequently asked the Center for the Study of the Presidency to take the lead in fleshing out the details of this innovative idea. After extensive consultations with communications professionals and Members of Congress, CSP proposed the Foundation for International Understanding (FIU), a grant-making public-private partnership that would support educational and entertainment media worldwide to encourage understanding across borders, cultures, and religions. This proposed foundation has been called "a Marshall Plan for the minds and spirits of the world's youth" by Ambassador Edward N. Ney.

> **The FIU has been called "a Marshall Plan for the minds and spirits of the world's youth."**

Taking advantage of the digital revolution and global interconnectedness, as described in Thomas Friedman's book *The World Is Flat*, the FIU would support the full range of communications media, from television and radio programming to Internet productions, mobile video content, and educational video games. The expansion of broadband Internet access and online virtual worlds presents especially promising opportunities to connect young people around the world for direct interaction and dialogue. Al-Qaeda and other terrorist organizations use new technologies to propagate their hate-filled ideologies; the FIU would use communication technologies as a force for good. Establishing the FIU in 2009, as the new administration and Congress arrive in Washington, would be an important step in demonstrating America's commitment to bridging divides in global tolerance and understanding.

Cultural and educational exchanges, which encourage cross-cultural understanding and empathy, comprise another important step in this direction. Prestigious exchange programs, including the Fulbright, Truman, and Marshall Scholars, remain invaluable and should receive more funding. Many current and past heads of state, beginning with the current President of France and Chancellor of Germany, participated in such exchanges in their younger years.

The crucial battle in the Middle East today is between the moderates and radicals. We need to take every opportunity to bolster the resources of the moderates. On this score, ironically, America has neglected its best weapon for our public strategy: the Muslim success story in America. Our Muslim community in many respects is flourishing. First, in this nation of religious tolerance, Islam is one of the most rapidly growing faiths. Second, Muslims are largely integrated and highly upwardly mobile. They participate in government. If there is any lack of balance in that community, it is the fact that theological institutions are not principally American funded, as are our Protestant, Catholic, and Jewish institutions. This means that some of those theological institutions are subjected to radicalization from overseas. Even with this imperfection, which can be remedied, the integration of American Muslims is

> America has neglected its best weapon for our public strategy: the Muslim success story in America.

in contrast to the many disaffected Muslims joining al-Qaeda and other related groups in Europe. Indeed, President Bush has good personal friends among the Muslim community. We have a great asset in the American Dream, and we need to figure out how to maintain it for the next generation.

Another major challenge is reimagining our presentation of the "the global war on terror." This issue has been raised continually by allies. As one NATO ambassador said, "we cannot lump all the worlds problems under the heading of "terrorism," especially since terrorism is not an ideology but rather a way of acting."[13] Even in the United States, some like Francis Fukuyama argue, "We are fighting hot counter-insurgency wars in Afghanistan and Iraq and against the national jihadist movement that we need to win, but conceiving the larger struggle as a global war, comparable to the World Wars or the Cold War, vastly overstates the problem, suggesting that we are taking on a large part of the Arab and Muslim worlds."[14] As previously mentioned, Zbigniew Brzezinski offers similar criticisms. We must clearly distinguish between fanatics who pursue extremist ends in the name of Islam and the more than one billion peaceful Muslims around the world.

For Americans, there is an argument that it may be worth calling the struggle of this generation something other than a "war." Europeans, with their longer experience of terrorism, have largely opted to change the American terminology to the "fight against terror," as Gordon Brown made clear when he recently met with George Bush at Camp David. Still, in America, war has often been used by political leaders—as in the war against cancer, or poverty, or drugs—to galvanize the public for an all-out, comprehensive national effort. In the Bush Administration, the term has unfortunately failed to have this effect. As we noted elsewhere, the nation was never really mobilized for the war on terror as if it were going to war. When the next President alters the terminology of this struggle—as he or she almost certainly will—it should be done carefully, and should not indicate a slackening, but rather an increase of national effort.

Another—perhaps the most difficult—element of America's public strategy is managing the spread of liberal democracy abroad. Americans have a tendency to believe in the inevitable spread of their values and principles—whether in the guise of Manifest Destiny, the empire of democracy, nation-building, or wars of liberation. As these examples suggest, there is a tenuous balance between American ideals and American power. When it comes to "democratization" of other nations, the first principle of American power ought to be close alignment with native allies. As Michael McFaul, a senior fellow at the Hoover Institution has said, "It is very, very, very rare that external actors play a direct role in democratization. . . . It's almost always through cooperating with domestic actors. They are the ones who are going to make democracy work or not, so those are the people we should be listening to in the way we make our foreign policy."[15] We forgot this truism in Iraq.

CHAPTER 11

OFFERING A VISION BEYOND WAR

I N HIS Second Inaugural Address, delivered on March 4, 1865, Abraham Lincoln laid out his vision of reconciling the North and South. The war was not yet over, but Lincoln was already focused on healing the country's wounds and rifts. Before V-J Day, Franklin Roosevelt's mind was likewise on a post-war world order. The fighting hadn't come close to ending when, in 1941, he obtained the agreement of twenty-six nations to take part in the "Declaration of United Nations," which formed the basis of the modern United Nations. Like Lincoln, Roosevelt also saw that reconstructing buildings, as well as a sense of trust, would require cooperation even with those who were still engaged in battle against one another. In July 1944, at Bretton Woods, New Hampshire, he convened the United Nations Monetary and Financial Conference, which created the International Monetary Fund and the International Bank for Reconstruction and Development. The work of these institutions laid the groundwork for the dollar-centered monetary system that persists to this day.

While fighting the war on terror, Bush offered his own "postwar" vision: a democratic Middle East, beginning with a transformed Iraq. As noble as this vision is, he has failed to heed the lessons of two similar Presidents—Woodrow Wilson, who sought to "make the world safe for democracy," and Lyndon

Johnson, who sought to make South Vietnam secure for democracy. Unfortunately, Bush allowed his diplomacy, strategy, and especially his management of the home front to rhyme with the mistakes of Wilson and Johnson.

The three Presidents failed to carry out their transforming visions, in part, for the same reasons: all were unable to maintain a bipartisan coalition on Capitol Hill, keep the nation united, and marshal the diverse advice and skilled personnel in executing ambitious designs. As chronicled in critical books and government reports, the Bush Administration failed to plan realistically for the Iraq reconstruction. Talented people within the Administration were often excluded in a way that caused the malfunctioning of the National Security Council (NSC) system. Not all of the necessary departments were brought in to planning sessions on Iraqi invasion and reconstruction. Often, strategy was left to policy-makers who imposed an ideologically idealized Iraq on a complicated and precarious reality.

Action for the Next President

The next President needs not only a vision for postwar Iraq, Afghanistan, and the broader Middle East but a pathway to achieve that vision. While Wilson, Johnson, and Bush lacked realistic designs for peace, Lincoln and Roosevelt did have such designs—though they died before being able to carry them out.

The next President will inherit the legacy of an Iraq being torn apart by a Sunni-Shi'ia civil war, Islamic extremism, and covert Iranian interventions. He or she will face a massive refugee crisis of at least two million Iraqis and perhaps Iranians by 2009. A more peaceful Iraq can only be achieved by carefully managing a U.S. drawdown, troop redeployment, and the recovery of our overstretched military. This military repositioning must be combined with candid consultation with all affected nations and states in the region and by the return of a U.S.-led coalition for restoring stability and peace to the region. Only a new President can pursue this kind of initiative, free of past errors and able to deal frankly with such vitally interested neighbors as Iran, Syria, Turkey, and the oil-rich Gulf states led by Saudi Arabia.

The next President will face daunting challenges in the Middle East, ranging from the Israel-Palestine

> The next President needs not just a vision for postwar Iraq, Afghanistan, and the broader Middle East; he or she needs a realistic pathway to achieve that vision.

conflict to the Sunni-Shi'ia rivalry as well as the contest between the moderate and radical members of the Islamic communities. One resource which could be used to help address and amend these fissures is the Organization of the Islamic Conference (OIC), which includes fifty-seven mostly Islamic nations from around the globe. The OIC's objectives are to promote "solidarity among all Islamic member states" and foster cooperation of economic, social, cultural, and scientific fields to eliminate racial discrimination and segregation, safeguard dignity, independence, social rights, and so forth.

This council could help to nurture home-grown reform movements, and at the very least ought to be encouraged as a source of legitimate and progressive authority in the Muslim World. It is significant that the OIC made an offer in the summer of 2007 for a contingent of peacekeeping troops to assist in such activities in Iraq with the inevitable drawdown of U.S. forces, although this offer was rejected by the Maliki leadership. While President Bush has begun to engage the OIC—agreeing recently to appoint an envoy to the organization for the purpose of "listening,"—the next President ought to expand U.S. cooperation with this and other multilateral institutions in the Middle East.

Another model for promoting reform while respecting the sovereignty of Muslim states can be found in a remarkable organization founded during the Cold War. Meeting in Helsinki in 1975, thirty-five heads of government, including President Gerald Ford and Soviet Premier Leonid Brezhnev, produced a list of agreements promising to protect the human rights of their citizens and undertake various forms of international cooperation. This was the first time the Soviets recognized the rights to free speech and travel. The so-called Final Act of this summit was to establish an ongoing Conference for Security and Cooperation in Europe (CSCE). Although the CSCE became an important tool in winning the Cold War, the organization accepted the Soviets because it recognized existing boarders. Even during intense periods of confrontation, including the Soviet deployment of SS-20 missiles as a weapon of blackmail, the CSCE worked across lines of conflict to foster productive cultural and scientific exchanges and to broaden radio broadcasts into Eastern Europe and the Soviet Union, which in effect chipped away at the Iron Curtain. With the fall of that curtain, the organization then turned into an instrument for democratization and human rights.

∾ Why not extend or re-create CSCE in the Middle East today?

Why not extend or re-create this institution in the Middle East today? Our former representatives to the CSCE, Ambassador Max Kampelman, suggested this idea to the Bush Administration to no avail, but the next President ought to take it up. Kampelman argued that "nonparticipant" CSCE members should be invited to be full voting members, thereby extending the Helsinki principles, including the humanitarian ones, beyond the strict geography of Europe and into the Middle East. It should be recognized that even today, in the midst of the Israeli-Palestinian conflict, scientific exchanges have been maintained through our universities and the National Academies, even with Iran. Such exchanges have occurred in science and technology between the Palestinian areas and Israel. Let's build on this opportunity and incorporate greater efforts into a larger conceptual framework for the entire Middle East modeled after the Helsinki initiative.

Thinking more ambitiously, the next President might also take on the most deadly threat to our nation and civilization: the nuclear one. The head of the International Atomic Energy Agency (IAEA), Muhammad ElBaradei, has ominously warned that although much attention is currently focused on North Korea and Iran, up to thirty countries could potentially develop nuclear capabilities in the coming years. In other words, the best efforts under current American and European policies might not stop a nuclear cascade. This stern warning helped to bring a diverse group of eminent American public servants together under the auspices of the Hoover Institution to call for a daring new approach to nuclear disarmament. George Shultz, William Perry, Henry Kissinger, Sam Nunn, and Kampelman argue that the United States can no longer rely on the older strategies of nuclear deterrence because terrorist groups do not react predictably to the threat of death.

The authors assert that the Cold War theory and practice of "mutually assured destruction" no longer applies and that new nuclear states do not have the benefit of a long history of implementing safeguards during the Cold War to prevent nuclear accidents, misjudgments, or unauthorized launches. Together with their political and scientific delegates, they "endorse setting the goal of a world free of nuclear weapons and working energetically on the actions required to achieve that goal," specifically by changing the Cold War posture of

∾ Why not a Reykjavick Two for the world?

deployed nuclear weapons, reducing the size of nuclear forces in all states, and halting the production of fissile material for weapons globally.[1*] The central idea behind this declaration is that the United States should be in the lead of developing the strategies to aim at accomplishing this visionary goal with allies and partners. Ambassador Kampelman, who attended the historic Reykjavik Summit where Reagan and Gorbachev made progress on intermediate-range missile disarmament, calls this initiative "Reykjavik Two."

Protecting America also means taking creative action at home. As Lincoln created the National Academies; as Roosevelt created the G.I. Bill of Rights; and as Dwight Eisenhower created the Highway Bill; so must our next President develop homeland security investments that create a better America. The concept of dual investments has not been defined or explained to the nation, at least to the extent that the Presidents above have done so. Dual investments support programs

---

* Even before this group, Max Kampelman has been a leader arguing for such a policy. He was a strategic negotiator at Reykjavik and shaped Reagan's hope to rid the world of nuclear weapons. But he also recognized Reagan's leverage with SDI, which provided an incentive to move the Soviets to genuine mutual productions of nuclear weapons. The challenge of implementing this proposal would be finding the leverage of a missile defense system which would "devalue" the weapons and could lead to a similar course of honest reduction and disarmament. The current AEGIS ballistic missile defense system would be the most logical course. According to the Missile Defense Agency, to date, sixteen Aegis Cruisers and Destroyers have been upgraded with the long-range surveillance and track capability needed to intercept potential threats. Of these, the engagement capability has been installed in three Aegis Cruisers and seven Destroyers. The capability was tactically certified in the summer of 2006. Other missile defense deployment options could be considered in this strategic reappraisal to build this type of leverage, this includes Space.

or technologies that have multiple benefits. Eisenhower's Highway Bill, for instance, was intended first to facilitate emergency deployment in the case of a nuclear attack, but did more to bolster interstate commerce than perhaps any other legislation of the twentieth century.

∽ **Dual investments support programs or technologies that have multiple benefits.**

The next President would do well to study Eisenhower's example, particularly at a time when the infrastructure of our towns and cities is deteriorating, leaving us exposed to devastating accidents such as the collapse of the Minneapolis Bridge on August 1, 2007, and inviting terrorist attacks.[*] More than perhaps any other policy insight, dual investment would help to move America from a sense of peril to a sense of promise.

In no field is this truer than public health, which voters have already determined to be the key domestic issue.[2] Public health concerns include soaring medical costs and uninsured citizens as well as the need to improve disease prevention and preparedness, protect against and respond to natural disasters, pandemics, and bioterrorist threats, and strengthen health-related research.[3][**] Despite spending over $2 trillion a year on

---

[*] When addressing the infrastructure issue one can refer to the Center for Strategic and International Studies comprehensive report on March 27, 2006. The Senate has passed the National Infrastructure Improvement Act of 2007. At this writing, it is still to be faced in the House.

[**] Rear Admiral Susan Blumenthal, M.D., CSP Senior Advisor for Health and Medicine, provides public health leadership in a wide variety of arenas, including analyzing new healthcare policies for the next Administration. Much of Dr. Blumenthal's contributions to this piece have been previously published. Two particular articles referenced throughout this section are, "Health Care and the 2008 Presidential Elections: A Window of Opportunity," and "Presidential Candidates' Prescriptions for a Healthier Future: A Side-by-Side Comparison."

healthcare—18 percent of the GDP and twice as much as any other nation—the United States ranks only forty-second in life expectancy[4] and thirty-seventh in a World Health Organization study on the performance of national health systems.[5] Tragically, 70 percent of these costs are linked to preventable factors such as smoking, obesity, lack of physical activity, and substance abuse.

Escalating public health expenditures affect America on every level . . . impacting our global competitiveness and national security.

These escalating expenditures affect America on every level, not only compromising the health of individuals, but impacting our global competitiveness and national security. Businesses are suffering from the rising health care costs of their employees. Many are forced to cut benefits, downsize, or move production overseas. Since September 11 and the anthrax attacks, the United States has spent billions of dollars on homeland security, public health infrastructure, health information technology systems, and response strategies. Yet, with the destruction caused by Hurricane Katrina and the possibility of a pandemic flu, the country faces an alarming reality—we remain underprepared for these threats.

Part of the problem is an outmoded belief that health is an exclusively domestic issue. But with 79 percent of all chronic diseases occurring in the developing world, the United States has an important role to play in sharing knowledge to help prevent and treat illnesses worldwide. In an increasingly interconnected global society in which an estimated two million people cross national borders every day, not even the wealthiest countries can protect themselves from bioterrorism or infectious diseases such as avian flu that may be just a jet plane away.[6]

In response to these threats, America must take steps now to modernize and coordinate its health care system. The next

Administration will need to build on current efforts in preventive medicine and health information technology as driving forces of health care reform. Coordinating government on these issues is also key. Currently, many important health concerns such as pandemic flu, natural disasters, AIDS, and obesity cross over forty-five federal departments and agencies, resulting in fragmentation and redundancy. In the final analysis, comprehensive healthcare reform will be needed. Such reform should address a number of dimensions including access, cost, quality, and personal responsibility.

To navigate this landscape and provide much-needed leadership, the next President ought to consider appointing a White House Health Advisor.

In addition to the national security, homeland security, and healthcare challenges discussed above, our nation faces a range of other key sustainability challenges that need to be addressed. These range from our underperforming K-12 education system, dependence on foreign oil, various environmental concerns, outdated immigrations policies, growing infrastructure concerns, and strained foreign relations just to name a few. All of these and other key challenges must be on the new President's radar screen.

CONCLUSION:
FROM PERIL TO PROMISE

FACED WITH grave threats, and serious sustainability challenges, our next President—and our next Strategist-in-Chief—has to move the nation away from this sense of peril to a sense of promise, just as Roosevelt did at the outset of the Depression and again toward the end of the Second World War.

If the next President wishes to follow Abraham Lincoln or Roosevelt's example, that President will have to think beyond Iraq and Afghanistan—even beyond the remaining pitfalls for homeland security. Granted, a fear factor is needed to deal with genuine danger, but as FDR warned, fear can be paralyzing. The art of our grand strategy must be to move from peril to promise, at home and abroad. The war on terror must not be an isolated campaign but must be an undertaking that impacts a range of national interests and activities; from education and health to the budgetary situation, regaining strategic control of our energy options, coordination of the homeland security apparatus, and the proper functioning of the national security process. Every move must add up to a promise of a truly better America and a better world.

It will take great courage to face the totality of our challenges at home and abroad. The next President will surely encounter political and bureaucratic opposition. The best way to defuse potential critics is to enlist them: creative minds from both parties ought to be involved in the strategy-making effort. Nonetheless, the work of building a grand strategy must commence soon. It might look like this:

∽ The next President must heed Lincoln's summons to think anew and act anew.

For the first 120 days, the next President should mandate an unparalleled overall net assessment of the nation's challenges at home and abroad. This must be a national call to action. Second, using this assessment, the President should devise a budgetary strategy to deal with competing near-term demands arising from our engagements overseas and the need to rebuild the military, as well as our long-term demands, including our failing schools, the looming Social Security and health crises, and inadequate support for basic scientific research.

From the beginning, Congress must be made a partner in this consensus-building endeavor, which should prominently involve leading members from both parties. The business community should be called in as well, ideally through the Business Roundtable, which could bring together prominent CEOs from industry leading corporations like Procter and Gamble, General Electric, and Microsoft, as well as representatives from smaller businesses. University presidents throughout our nation, including those at land grant institutions should be included. The same call should be made on medical centers such as Cleveland Clinic and Johns Hopkins. Another major partner in this net assessment should be the National Academies, which joined forces two years ago to issue an important report on science and math

---

* The National Academies comprise four organizations—the National Academy of Sciences, the National Academy of Engineering, the Institute of Medicine and the National Research Council.

education, *The Gathering Storm.*[*] Private foundations and policy institutions should be marshaled as well. In the field of health, the Commonwealth Foundation of New York should draw on its experience in compiling a study of the best worldwide health practices. In all cases,

> ∽ **Who should lead this critical reassessment of the nation's challenges?**

participants should explore alternative and contingent scenarios and focus particularly on "force-multiplier" breakthroughs which have application across more than one area.

Who should lead this critical undertaking? One contender could be the Comptroller General in the Government Accountability Office, an office currently held by David M. Walker. He brings sober understanding of the budgetary realities we face, and he holds a fifteen-year appointment.[*] In an effort to devise strategic, bipartisan solutions to these challenges, Walker has reached out to policy institutions, as he has done in the Fiscal Wake-up Tour, which involves the Concord Coalition, Brookings Institution, and Heritage Foundation. His perspective offers a point of departure, but it needs political support and public momentum.

Another coconvener could be Norman Augustine, who has chaired reports for the National Academy and has experience as an outstanding corporate CEO. This unmatched national project would prepare the President to rally around action plans. A candid net assessment may mean putting members of

---

The National Academies bring together committees of experts in all areas of scientific and technological endeavor as a public service to the nation. These experts serve pro bono to address critical national issues and give advice to the federal government and the public.

[*] David M. Walker should be commended for his insightful analysis within the document, *GAO Forces That Will Shape America's Future: Themes from GAO's Strategic Plan.*

Congress and the Administration in tough political situations. For that reason, it might be wise to follow the voting model laid out in the Bases Realignment and Closing Commission of 2005, which Congress voted on as a package, so avoiding individual votes on controversial items. Instead of a first 100 days similar to Roosevelt or Johnson, there could be a first 120 days to put into place the grand strategy. As a part of this endeavor, a commission has already been proposed to recommend legislation addressing our nation's unsustainable long-term fiscal outlook.*

The next President will face long odds, but we have been there before. Within the last 250 years, we have launched a new nation, preserved the Union in the Civil War, and faced down tyranny in World War II and the Cold War. Just prior to the Civil War a spent President James Buchanan was unwilling and unable to cope with the impending threat to the Union. He could not lead. The next President cannot be a Buchanan. The next President has no choice—he or she must heed Lincoln's summons:

> The dogmas of the quiet past are inadequate to the stormy present. The occasion is piled high with difficulty, and we must rise—with the occasion. As our case is new,

---

*The legislative initiative was taken by Congressmen Frank Wolf (R-VA) and Jim Cooper (D-TN) and Senators Judd Gregg (R-NH), Kent Conrad (D-ND), and George Voinovich (R-OH) and has the endorsement of the Concord Coalition. This legislation would require Congress to address the nation's looming fiscal crisis before spending on Social Security, Medicare, and Medicaid bankrupts the government. Congress would vote up or down on a plan to overhaul spending and revenue, as drafted by a sixteen-member, bipartisan commission made of members of Congress and outside appointees of the Legislative and Executive branches.

so we must think anew, and act anew. We must disenthrall ourselves, and then we shall save our country. Fellow-citizens, we cannot escape history. We of this Congress and this Administration, will be remembered in spite of ourselves. No personal significance, or insignificance, can spare one or another of us. The fiery trial through which we pass, will light us down, in honor or dishonor, to the latest generation. . . . We shall nobly save, or meanly lose, the last best hope of earth.[1]

Our next President can meet this call to greatness.

Our next President must begin with uniting a divided America to write a great new chapter in American history.

ACKNOWLEDGMENTS

I OWE MANY grateful thanks to Trustee Stanley Zax for challenging me to undertake this project and Trustees David Gergen and Max Kampelman who enhanced this piece greatly by providing thoughtful and in-depth introductions. Thank you to Margot Connor, who was the indefatigable and patient preparer of numerous drafts, and to Louisa Thomas and Justin Reynolds, who as a team reshaped my drafts into more understandable form and painfully prevailed in condensing my lengthy ramblings. I thank longtime colleagues, Marshall Wright and Richard Whalen, for their wise and thorough suggestions on presentation and substance. I thank the many minds within CSP, which have helped in various ways including Limor Ben-Har, Rear Admiral Susan J. Blumenthal, M.D., M.P.A. (ret.), John Boyer, Alex Douville, Sarah Ficenec, Job Henning, Meghann King, Thomas Kirlin, Ambassador Gary Matthews, Corazon Mendoza, Ed Rowe, Stephanie Safdi, Elise Schlissel, Emily Shaftel, Anne Solomon, and Jeffrey Thomas. Outside of CSP, I owe thanks to those who reviewed this book and provided their astute suggestions including Al Felzenberg, Paul Neely, Landon Parvin, Rudy Penner, James Pfiffner, Evan Thomas,

Jeanette and Paul Wagner, John Yochelson, and Al Zapanta. I especially appreciate the review of George Edwards. Finally, the advice and additions of U.S. Comptroller General David M. Walker were tremendously encouraging and appreciated. I hold myself entirely accountable for the views expressed in this book.

October 1, 2007
David M. Abshire

ABOUT THE CENTER FOR THE STUDY OF THE PRESIDENCY

Mission

Promote leadership in the Presidency and the Congress to generate innovative solutions to current national challenges;

Preserve the historic memory of the Presidency by identifying the lessons from the successes and failures of such leadership;

Draw on a wide range of talent to offer ways to better organize an increasingly compartmentalized federal government;

Educate and inspire the next generation of American's leaders to incorporate civility, inclusiveness, and character into their public and private lives and discourse.

Contact information: The Center for the Study of the Presidency, 1029 19th Street, NW, Suite 250, Washington, D.C. 20036. Telephone: 202-872-9800. Fax: 202-872-9811. Web: www.thepresidency.org

ABOUT THE AUTHOR

DAVID M. ABSHIRE is president of the Center for the Study of the Presidency and President of the Richard Lounsbery Foundation, which focuses on science and education. He is Vice Chairman of the Board of the Center for Strategic and International Studies (CSIS) which he cofounded in 1962, initially as a part of Georgetown University and since 1987 an independent institution. He headed CSIS for over three decades. He also cofounded, with Dr. Kazuo Inamori, the CSIS Abshire-Inamori Leadership Academy.

Dr. Abshire is a 1951 graduate of West Point and was decorated during the Korean War as a company commander. He received his Ph.D. in History from Georgetown University, where for many years he served as an adjunct professor. His full-time government service includes Congressional staff (1958–1960), assistant secretary of state for Congressional Relations (1970–1973), U.S. Ambassador to NATO (1983–1987), and in the Presidential Cabinet as special counselor to President Reagan in early 1987. His part-time government service has included service on the Advisory Board of the Naval War College (1973–1974), as the first chairman of the Board for International Broadcasting (1975–1977), member of the Murphy Commission (1974–1975), the President's Foreign Intelligence Advisory Board (1981–1982), the President's

Task Force on U.S. Governmental International Broadcasting (1991), and the Advisory Commission for Public Diplomacy mandated by Congress (2003). Dr. Abshire is currently a member of the Department of Homeland Security Advisory Council Academe, Policy & Research Senior Advisory Committee. In 2005, he was the Chairman of the Sea Domain for the Task Force on Preventing the Entry of Weapons of Mass Effect Into the United States that reported its findings to the Secretary of Homeland Security in January 2006.

He served for nine years on the Board of Procter and Gamble and headed its first Public Policy Committee. He is a trustee of the George C. Marshall Foundation and the Advisory Boards of America Abroad, Layalina Productions, Mount Vernon and the St. Albans School of Public Service. He is also a cofounder of the Trinity National Leadership Roundtable.

He has been decorated by seven heads of government and received four honorary degrees. The author of six books, *The South Rejects a Prophet*, 1967; *International Broadcasting: A New Dimension of Western Diplomacy*, 1976; *Foreign Policy Makers: President vs. Congress*, 1979; *Preventing World War III: A Realistic Grand Strategy*, 1988; *Putting America's House in Order: The Nation as a Family*, with Brock Brower; and *Saving the Reagan Presidency: Trust Is the Coin of the Realm*, 2005. He is also editor of *Triumphs and Tragedies of the Modern Presidency: Seventy-Six Case Studies in Presidential Leadership*.

NOTES

Chapter 1

1. Karen DeYoung and Walter Pincus, "Al-Qaeda's Gains Keep U.S. at Risk, Report Says," *Washington Post*, July 18, 2007.

2. Paul M. Kennedy, *The Rise and Fall of the Great Powers: Economic Change and Military Conflict from 1500 to 2000* (New York: Random House, 1987).

3. Edward Gibbon, *History of the Decline and Fall of the Roman Empire* (New York: Modern Library, 2003).

4. Thucydides, *History of the Peloponnesian War* (New York: Penguin, 1986).

5. For the full text, see "First Inaugural Address of Abraham Lincoln" at www.yale.edu/lawweb/avalon/presiden/inaug/lincoln1.htm.

6. David M. Abshire, ed., *Triumphs and Tragedies of the Modern Presidency: Seventy-Six Case Studies in Presidential Leadership* (Washington, DC: Praeger Publishers, 2001).

7. David M. Abshire, ed., *In Harm's Way: Intervention and Prevention* (Washington, DC: Praeger Publishers, 2000).

8. Thomas M. Kirlin, ed., *Advancing Innovation: Improving the S&T Advisory Structure and Policy Process* (Washington, DC: Praeger Publishers, 2000). Cosponsored by the American Association for the Advancement of Science.

9. Max Farrand, ed. *The Records of the Federal Convention of 1787* (New Haven and London: Yale University Press, 1937), Rev. ed. 4 vols.

Chapter 2

1. Gordon S. Wood, *Revolutionary Characters: What Made the Founders Different* (New York: Penguin Press, 2006), pp. 35–36.
2. David M. Abshire, *The Character of George Washington* (Washington, DC: CSP, 1998).

Chapter 3

1. Douglas Southall Freeman, *George Washington: A Biography* (New York: Charles Scribner's Sons, 1948), vol. 3, pp. 19–41.
2. Ronald Chernow, *Alexander Hamilton* (New York: Penguin Press, 2004), p. 326.
3. George Washington's Farewell Address from the Avalon Project at Yale Law School (www.yale.edu/lawweb/avalon/washing.htm)
4. George Washington to Moses Seixas, August 21, 1790.
5. For the text, see "Monroe Doctrine; December 2, 1823," at www.yale.edu/lawweb/avalon/monroe.htm.
6. Arthur M. Schlesinger Jr., *Age of Jackson* (Boston: Little, Brown and Company, 1945).
7. Jeffrey B. Morris and Richard Morris, Ed., *Encyclopedia of American History* (New York: Harper Collins, 1996), p. 215.
8. M. McPherson, *To the Best of My Ability* (New York: DK Publishing, Inc., 2000), p. 116.
9. Doris Kearns Goodwin, *Team of Rivals: The Political Genius of Abraham Lincoln* (New York: Simon & Schuster, 2005), p. xvii.
10. For the text, see "Second Inaugural Address of Abraham Lincoln" at www.yale.edu/lawweb/avalon/presiden/inaug/lincoln2.htm.
11. David Herbert Donald, *Lincoln* (New York: Random House, 1995), pp. 302–4. Jacob K Jabits, *Who Makes War* (New York: William Morrow and Co Inc, 1973), p. 130
12. David Herbert Donald, *Lincoln* (New York: Random House, 1995), pp. 362–63.
13. Leo Tolstoy, *The World* (New York, 1909).
14. Karl Rove, Letter to David M. Abshire, 2006.

15. Steven C. Gravlin, "*Maine*, Sinking of the USS," in John Whiteclay Chambers II, ed. *The Oxford Companion to American Military History* (New York: Oxford University Press, 1999), p. 410.

16. Warren Zimmerman, *First Great Triumph: How Five Americans Made Their Country A World Power* (New York: Farrar, Straus and Giroux, October 2002), pp. 434–35.

17. John Milton Cooper, *Triumphs and Tragedies of the Modern Presidency: Seventy-Six Case Studies in Presidential Leadership* (Washington, DC: Praeger Publishers, 2001). Cooper is also author of the latest major study on this subject: *Breaking the Heart of the World: Woodrow Wilson and the fight over the League of Nations* (Cambridge: Cambridge University Press, 2001).

18. James MacGregor Burns, "Roosevelt's First One Hundred Days," in *Triumphs and Tragedies of the Modern Presidency: Seventy-Six Case Studies in Presidential Leadership* (Washington, DC: Praeger Publishers, 2001), pp. 20-21.

19. *Schechter Poultry Corp. v. United States*, 295 U.S. 495 (1935).

20. Arthur S. Link, *American Epoch: A History of the United States Since the 1890s* (New York: Alfred A. Knopf), p. 425.

21. Warren F. Kimball, "Franklin D. Roosevelt and World War II," *Presidential Studies Quarterly*, March 2004, vol. 34, No. 1, pp. 83-99.

22. Roberta Wohlstetter, *Pearl Harbor: Warning and Decision* (Stanford, CA: Stanford University Press, 1967).

23. Edward S. Corwin, *The President: Office and Powers, 1789–1957* (New York: New York University Press, 1957).

24. David Abshire, *Saving the Reagan Presidency* (College Station: Texas A&M University Press, 2005).

25. G. Pascal Zachary, *Endless Frontier: Vannevar Bush, Engineer of the American Century* (New York: Free Press, 1997).

26. David McCullough, *Truman* (New York: Simon & Schuster, 1992), pp. 991–92.

27. Geoffrey Perret, "The 1956 Federal Highway Act," in *Triumphs and Tragedies of the Modern Presidency: Seventy-Six Case Studies in Presidential Leadership* (Washington, DC: Praeger Publishers, 2001), p. 81.

28. For the text of the speech, "Eisenhower's farewell address" see http://en.wikisource.org/wiki/Eisenhower%27s_farewell_address.

29. Fred I. Greenstein, *Hidden-Hand Presidency: Eisenhower as a Leader* (New York: Basic Books Inc., 1982).

30. For the text of the inaugural speech, see "Inaugural Address of President John F. Kennedy" at www.jfklibrary.org/Historical +Resources/Archives/Reference+Desk/Speeches/JFK/003POF03 Inaugural01201961.htm.

31. Barbara W. Tuchman, *Guns of August* (New York: Macmillan, 1962).

32. Lewis Sorley, *A Better War: The Unexamined Victories and Final Tragedy of America's Last Years in Vietnam* (New York: Harcourt Brace & Company, 1999).

33. Egil Krogh, "The Break-in that History Forgot," *New York Times*, June 30, 2007.

34. Daniel Patrick Moynihan, *The American Experience* (New Haven: Yale University Press, December 1999).

35. CSP advisor, George Lardner, is completing an excellent book on the subject.

36. Gerald R. Ford, *A Time to Heal: The Autobiography of Gerald R. Ford* (New York: Harper & Row, 1979).

37. Gerald R. Ford, U.S. President. Address to Joint Session of Congress (April 10, 1975). *A Time to Heal* (New York: Harper & Row 1979), p. 254.

38. Jimmy Carter, "Interview with Jimmy Carter," *Carter Presidency Project*, November 29, 1982: 7–66.

39. Zbignew Brzezinski, *Power and Principle: Memoirs of the National Security Adviser, 1977–1981* (New York: Farrar, Straus & Giroux, 1983).

40. Fred I. Greenstein, *The Presidential Difference: Leadership Style from FDR to George W. Bush.* Second Edition (Princeton, NJ: Princeton University Press, 2004), p. 141.

41. James McGregor Burns, *Running Alone: Presidential Leadership— from JFK to Bush II: Why It Has Failed and How We Can Fix It* (New York: Basic Books, 2006), p. 112.

42. Rudolph G. Penner, "The National Economic Council and the Economic Policy Board," in *Triumphs and Tragedies of the Modern Presidency: Seventy-Six Case Studies on Presidential Leadership* (Washington, DC: Praeger Paperback, 2001), p. 131.

43. David M. Abshire, *Saving the Reagan Presidency: Trust Is the Coin of the Realm* (College Station: Texas A&M University Press, 2005), p. 176.

44. George Edwards, "The Balanced Budget Act of 1997," in *Triumphs and Tragedies of the Modern Presidency: Seventy-Six Case Studies in Presidential Leadership* (Washington, DC: Praeger Publishers, 2001).

45. William J. Clinton, "Remarks and an Exchange with Reporters Following a Meeting with Congressional Leaders," *The American Presidency Project,* July 15, 1993.

46. Stephen Barr, "Transforming FEMA," *Triumphs and Tragedies of the Modern Presidency: Seventy-Six Case Studies in Presidential Leadership,* David Abshire, Ed. (Westport, CT, and London: Praeger, 2001), pp. 268–70.

47. David Abshire, "Prologue," *Triumphs and Tragedies of the Modern Presidency: Seventy-six Case Studies in Presidential Leadership,* Ed. David Abshire (Westport, CT: Praeger Publishers, 2001), p. xiii.

48. For the full text, see "Inaugural Address of George W. Bush; January 20, 2001," at www.yale.edu/lawweb/avalon/presiden/inaug/gbush1.htm.

49. Richard Cohen, "Bush the Neoliberal," *Washington Post*, May 29, 2007.

50. George W Bush, White House Rose Garden, Office of the Press Secretary, May 30, 2007, President Bush Announces Five-Year, $30 Billion HIV/AIDS Plan.

51. Scott Shane, "Recent Flexing of Presidential Powers Had Personal Roots in Ford White House," *The New York Times*, December 30, 2006.

52. James McGregor Burns, *Running Alone: Presidential Leadership—From JFK to Bush II: Why It Has Failed and How We Can Fix It* (New York: Basic Books, 2006), p. 168.

53. Barton Gellman and Jo Becker, "A Different Understanding with the President," *Washington Post*, June 24, 2007.

54. John Lewis Gaddis, *Surprise, Security and the American Experience* (Cambridge, Mass.: Harvard University Press, 2004), p. 86.

55. Louis Fisher, "Introduction," *Presidential Studies Quarterly* (Malden, MA: Blackwell Publishing, June 2004) 33(3): 463–65.

56. Louis Fisher, *Presidential Powers* (Lawrence: University of Kansas Press, 2004), pp. 208, 211.

57. George C. Edwards, and Desmond S. King, eds. *The Polarized Presidency of George W. Bush* (New York: Oxford University Press, 2007), pp. 245–46.

58. Ibid.

59. Jim Rutenberg and Carl Hulse, "President's Push on Immigration Tests G.O.P. Base," *New York Times*, June 3, 2007.

60. Center for the Study of the Presidency, *Declaration of Civility and Inclusive Leadership* (Washington, DC: CSP, 2006).

61. 9/11 Public Discourse Project, www.9-11pdp.org/about/index .htm.

62. Alvin S. Felzenberg, *Governor Tom Kean: From the New Jersey Statehouse to the 9-11 Commission* (New Jersey: Rutgers University Press, 2006), p. 437.

63. Report to the President, March 31, 2005. Introduction, Commission on the Intelligence Capabilities of the United States Regarding Weapons of Mass Destruction.

64. Congressman Frank Wolf, Press Conference, Senate Arms Services Hearing Room, United States Capitol, March 15, 2006.

65. Amy Zegart, "Blue Ribbons, Black Boxes: Toward a Better Understanding of Presidential Commissions," *Presidential Studies Quarterly*, June 2004, vol. 34, No. 2, pp. 366–93.

Chapter 4

1. *Youngstown Co. v. Sawyer*, 343 U.S. 579 (1952).

2. Edward S. Corwin, *The President: Office and Powers, 1789–1957* (New York: New York University Press, 1957).

Chapter 5

1. Isaiah Berlin, *The Hedgehog and the Fox* (New York: George Weidenfeld & Nicolson, Ltd., 1953).

2. Michael E. Porter, *Competitive Strategy: Techniques for Analyzing Industries and Competitors* (New York: Free Press, 1980).

3. Each, in their own way, seeks the mantle of George Kennan, author of the United States Cold War containment doctrine, the last truly comprehensive American strategy.

4. Francis Fukuyama, *America at the Crossroads: Democracy, Power, and the Neoconservative Legacy* (New Haven, Conn.: Yale University Press, 2006).

5. Dennis Ross, *Statecraft: And How to Restore America's Standing in the World* (New York: Farrar, Straus & Giroux, 2007).

6. Anne-Marie Slaughter, *The Idea That Is America: Keeping Faith with Our Values in a Dangerous World* (New York: Basic Books, 2007).

7. Zbigniew Brzezinski, *Second Chance: Three Presidents and the Crisis of American Superpower* (New York: Basic Books, 2007).

8. This quote is very famous and Dr. Abshire wonders if it is necessary to cite.

9. Joseph S. Nye, *Soft Power: The Means to Success in World Politics* (New York: Public Affairs, 2004).

10. Sun Tzu, *The Art of War*, transl. Samuel B. Griffith (New York: Oxford University Press, 1963).

Chapter 6

1. http://homeland.cq.com/hs/flatfiles/temporaryItems/20070801 -1nrf-framework.pdf.

2. Dr. Ashton B. Carter and William J. Perry, Preventative Defense Project, meeting, April 19, 2007; and Ashton B. Carter, William J. Perry, and Michael M. May, "After the Bomb," *New York Times*, June 12, 2007.

Chapter 7

1. Perhaps some of the most informative are books on this subject are Thomas E. Ricks, *Fiasco: The American Military Adventure in Iraq* (New York: Penguin Press, July 2007); Rajiv Chandrasekaran, *Imperial Life in the Emerald City: Inside Iraq's Green Zone* (New York: Vintage, September 2007); George Packer, *The Assassin's Gate* (New York: Farrar, Straus and Giroux, 2005); and Michael R. Gordon

and General Bernard E. Trainor, *Cobra II* (New York: Pantheon Books, 2006).

2. "The Eisenhower Institute," Gettysburg College, www.eisenhowerinstitute.org.

Chapter 8

1. Warren Zimmerman, *First Great Triumph: How Five Americans Made Their Country A World Power* (New York: Farrar, Straus and Giroux, October 2002), pp. 434–35.

2. White House Press Release, May 15, 2007.

3. Bryan Bender, "West Point grads exit service at high rate," *Boston Globe*, April 11, 2007.

4. Carl von Clausewitz, *On War*, edited and translated by Michael Howard and Peter Paret (Princeton, NJ: Princeton University Press, 1976).

5. Eliot A. Cohen, *Supreme Command: Soldiers, Statesmen, and Leadership in Wartime* (New York: Free Press, 2002).

6. David Petraeus, "Battling for Baghdad," *Washington Post*, September 26, 2004.

7. General John Shalikashvili, *Joint Vision 2010* (Joint Chiefs of Staff: Department of Defense, 1996).

8. Committee on Department of Defense Basic Research, Division on Engineering and Physical Sciences, *Assessment of Department of Defense Basic Research*, National Research Council of The National Academies (Washington, DC: National Academies Press, 2005), p. 19.

9. Newt Gingrich, *Winning the Future: A 21st Century Contract with America* (Washington, DC: Regnery Publishing, 2005), p. 151.

10. More information on the Broad Foundation's *Strong American Schools* can be found at strongamericanschools.org.

Chapter 9

1. *Comprehensive Strategic Reform: Panel Report for the President and Congress* (Washington, DC: CSP, September 2001).

Chapter 10

1. P. X. Kelly, "War Crimes in the White House," Op Ed, *Washington Post*, July 26, 2007.

2. Thomas L. Friedman, *The World Is Flat: A Brief History of the Twenty-first Century* (New York: Farrar, Straus & Giroux, 2005).

3. Alexander Hamilton, John Jay, and James Madison, *The Federalist: A Commentary on the Constitution of the United States* (New York: Random House, 2001), p. 337.

4. For the full text, see "Gettysburg Address," at www.yale.edu/lawweb/avalon/gettyb.htm.

5. For the full text of Dr. King's "I Have a Dream" Address, see www.stanford.edu/group/King/publications/speeches/address_at_march_on_washington.pdf.

6. For the full text of the second inaugural address, see www.whitehouse.gov/news/releases/2005/01/20050120-1.html.

7. "Muslim Public Opinion on U.S. Policy, Attacks on Civilians and al-Qaeda," report from the Program on International Policy Attitudes at the University of Maryland, April 24, 2007, p. 5.

8. Ibid., p. 4.

9. "Rising Environmental Concern in 47-Nation Survey: Global Unease with Major World Powers," report from the Pew Global Attitudes Project, June 27, 2007, p. 22.

10. "Europe's Muslims More Moderate: The Great Divide: How Westerners and Muslims View Each Other," in *Conflicting Views in a Divided World*, Pew Global Attitudes Project, June 22, 2006, p. 32.

11. "Muslim Americans: Middle Class and Mostly Mainstream, War on Terror Concerns," report from the Pew Research Center, May 22, 2007, p. 54.

12. 12. Edward P. Djerejian, chairman, *Changing Minds, Winning Peace: A New Strategic Direction for U.S. Public Diplomacy in the Arab & Muslim World* (Report on the Advisory Group on Public Diplomacy for the Arab and Muslim World, 2003).

13. Ambassador Dominicus Struye De Swielanden, Defense College, Rome, November 19, 2004.

14. Francis Fukuyama, *America at the Crossroads: Democracy, Power, and the Neoconservative Legacy* (New Haven, Conn.: Yale University Press, 2006), p. 184.

15. Michael Coleman, "Iran's Detention of Scholars Spurs Debate Over Democracy Promotion," *Washington Diplomat*, August 2007.

Chapter 11

1. *Wall Street Journal*, January 11, 2007; and *New York Times*, April 24, 2006.

2. "Kaiser Health Tracking Poll: Election 2008—June 2007," Kaiser Family Foundation, June 20, 2007.

3. Susan Blumenthal, "Health Care and the 2008 Presidential Elections: A Window of Opportunity," *Huffington Post*, March 14, 2007; and Susan Blumenthal, J. B. Rubin, M. E. Treseler, J. Lin, and D. Mattos, "Presidential Candidates' Prescriptions for a Healthier Future: A Side-by-Side Comparison," *Huffington Post*, July 9, 2007.

4. National Center for Health Statistics and U.S. Census Bureau.

5. "Health Systems Performance Assessment," World Health Organization.

6. Susan Blumenthal and Elise Schlissel, "Health Diplomacy: A Currency for Peace," *Washington Times*, August 26, 2007.

Conclusion

1. Abraham Lincoln, Annual Message to Congress, December 1, 1862. For the full text, see www.teachingamericanhistory.org/library/index.asp?document=1065.

INDEX

Abizaid, John, 118, 133
Abraham Lincoln and the Second American Revolution (McPherson), 28, 152
Abrams, Creighton, Jr., 57
Absher, Michael, 46
Adams, John, 20, 22, 42
Adams, John Quincy, 25
Addison, Joseph, 14
Afghanistan, 4, 7, 45, 87, 103, 111, 120, 127, 133, 136, 158, 171
Age of Jackson (Schlesinger, Jr.), 25
Alexander the Great, 106, 107
alliances, ix, 3, 72, 104, 105; NATO, vii, 7, 11, 40, 43, 61, 67, 69–70, 80, 110, 120–21, 135–36, 158; SEATO, 52; Western, 72
Amendment: Cooper-Church, 57–58; Fifteenth, 31; First, 21; Twenty-fourth, 53
America at the Crossroads (Fukuyama), 108
Annihilation from Within: The Ultimate Threat to Nations (Iklé), 117
anthrax crisis, 115, 168
Ash Commission. *See* Presidential Advisory Council on Executive Organization
Ash, Roy, 55
Al-Askari Mosque bombing, 133

atomic bomb. *See* nuclear weapons
Augustine, Norman, 127, 129, 173
Avery, Sewell, 125

Baghdad, 73, 98, 110
Baker-Hamilton Iraq Study Group (ISG), 57, 92–93, 128, 132
Baker, James III, 44, 66, 72, 75, 92
"The Balanced Budget Act of 1997" (Edwards), 77
Balkan, 7, 80, 104, 121
Bay of Pigs, 12, 41, 51, 67, 98
Belfer Center for Science and International Affairs, 116
Ben-Gurion, David, 132
Beschloss, Michael, viii, 53
The Best and the Brightest (Halberstam), 52
Blumenthal, Susan, 167
Bonaparte, Napoleon, 17, 106, 110
Brezhnev, Leonid, 164
Broadcasting Board of Governors, 150
Broad, Eli, 141
Brock, Bill, 82, 156
Brookings Institution, 84, 173
Brooks, David, 74
Brown, Gordon, 115, 158
Bryan, William Jennings, 32
Brzezinski, Zbigniew, 63, 73, 108, 158